I0489951

Juest Check Comics
Comics
Vol. I

ADULT
CONTENT

KAREN "KACY JEY" JACOBS

ISBN:9798389360235

DEDICATION

I dedicate this book to all the folks living, visiting and thriving on Mustang Island, in the city of Port Aransas, Texas. To my many friends across the world, thank you. Special thanks to my kids, Josh, Dustin, Zack and Lauren Carter and to Wm Reid Means and his family, who are all supportive of my crazy.

INTRODUCTION

I moved to Port Aransas in January 2021, unknowing and unprepared for the world I staggered into.

Our island is all about fishing, beach bumming, live music revelry and friendly characters. The first time I struck up a conversation at the best local dive bar, Shorty's, and the folks there found out I moved to live and work on the island, they accepted me as a local, part of the crew. It's a small island and a pirate's paradise.

Being on this island is a different experience than anywhere I've been or lived. In Port Aransas on Mustang Island it's as if we are enveloped in a protective bubble, surrounded by a moat of salt water full of sharks, stingrays and yummy fish. We are separate from the world beyond our shores.

After living on the island for a few months, we all find it hard to leave. When we do, we can't wait to get home, to our little, not so private, escape from the world.

In the summer, the number of people on the island swells from 2,900 resident (as of 2020 Census) to hundreds of thousands of vacationers. Our couple dozen or so food establishments and the handful of bars are overwhelmed, but for the most part, it's all good vibes and great times. Hey, they're on vacation. Proportionally, compared to other places I've bartended, this gig is awesome, entertaining and different every day.

My "Juest Check Comics" are a little slice of this life on our Island.

Karen "Kacy Jey" Jacobs

JUEST CHECK COMICS

Date	Table	Guests	Server	
2022		All	KJ	50567

APPT—SOUP/SAL—ENTREE—VEG/POT—DESSERT—BEV

Port Aransas:
A SMALL
Drinking Island
With a Fishing
Problem

		Tax	
		Total	

MADE IN THE USA

Guest Receipt

Date	Amount	Guests	
			50567

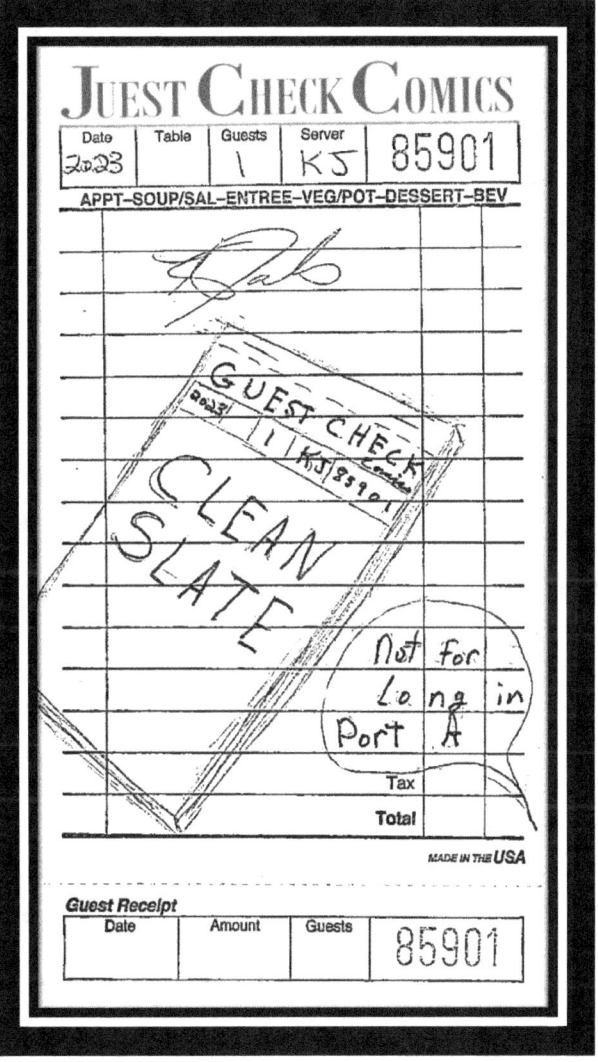

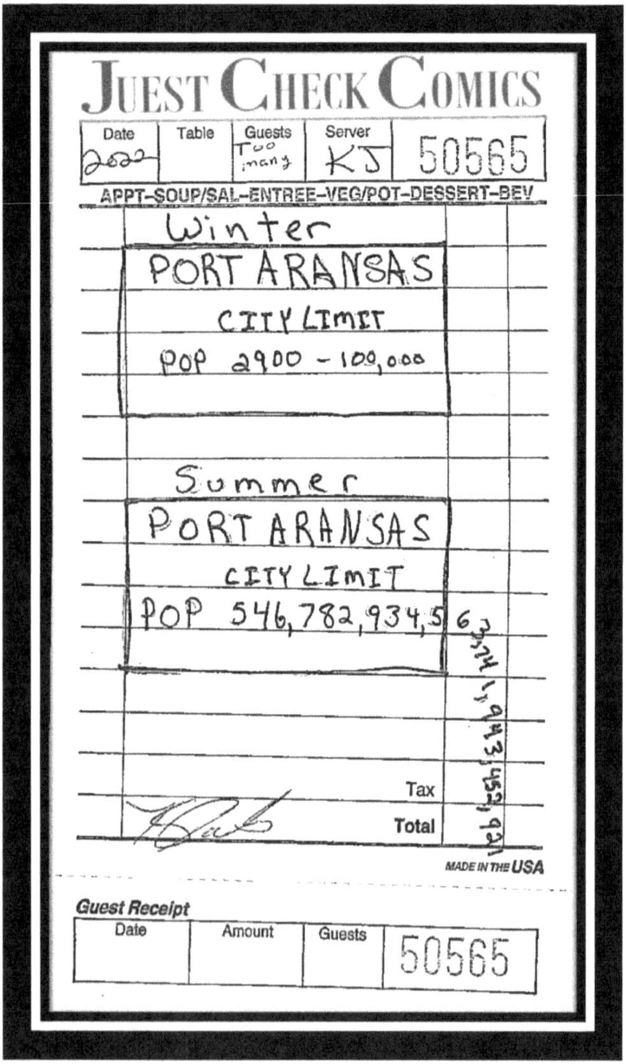
JUEST CHECK COMICS
Date
2022
Table
Guests
Too many
Server
KJ
50565
APPT–SOUP/SAL–ENTREE–VEG/POT–DESSERT–BEV
Winter
PORT ARANSAS
CITY LIMIT
POP 2900 - 100,000
Summer
PORT ARANSAS
CITY LIMIT
POP 546,782,934,56,374,1,943,452,921
Tax
Total
MADE IN THE USA
Guest Receipt
Date
Amount
Guests
50565

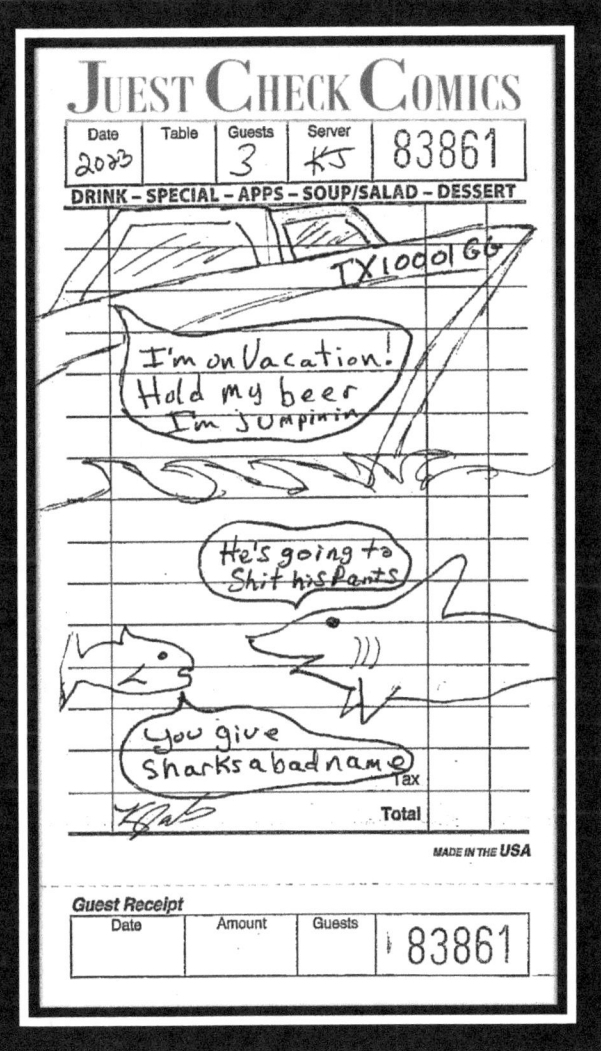

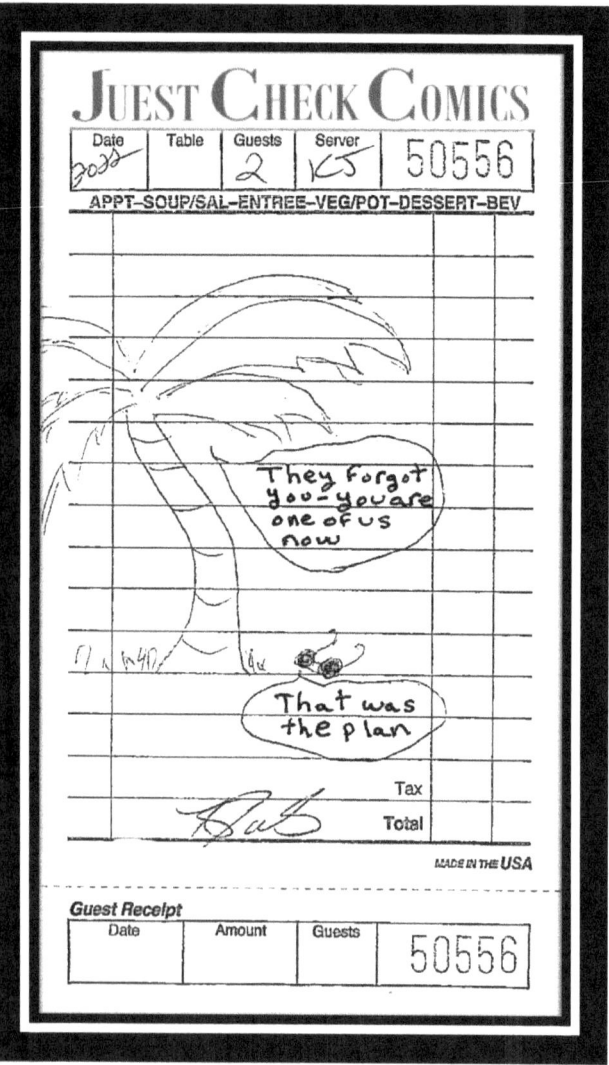

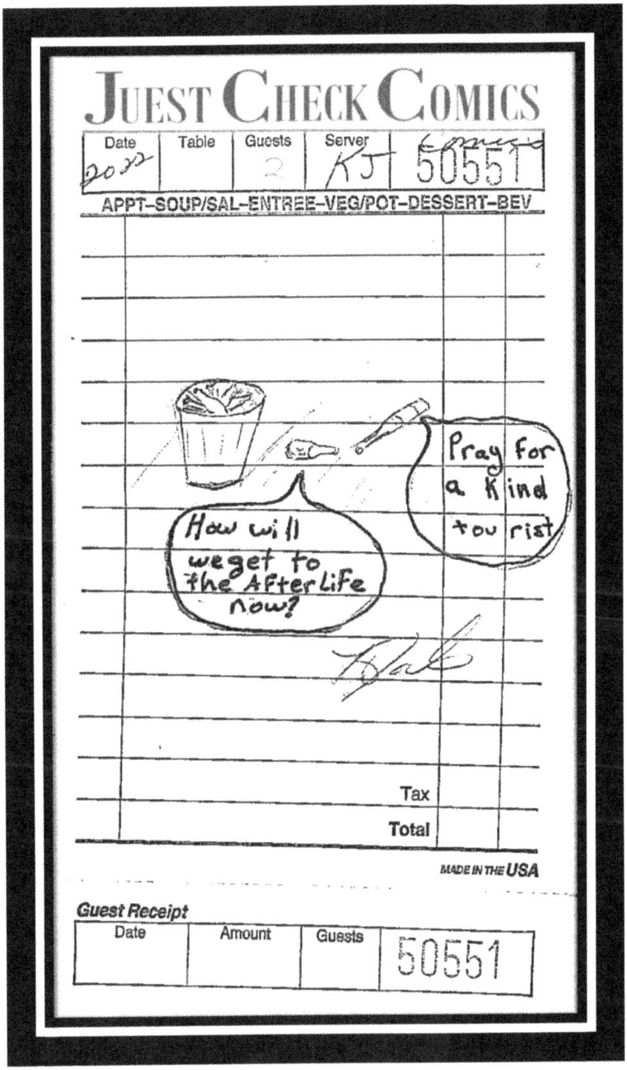
JUEST CHECK COMICS
Date
Table
Guests
2
Server
KJ
50551
APPT–SOUP/SAL–ENTREE–VEG/POT–DESSERT–BEV
Pray for a Kind tourist
How will we get to the AfterLife now?
Tax
Total
MADE IN THE USA
Guest Receipt
Date
Amount
Guests
50551

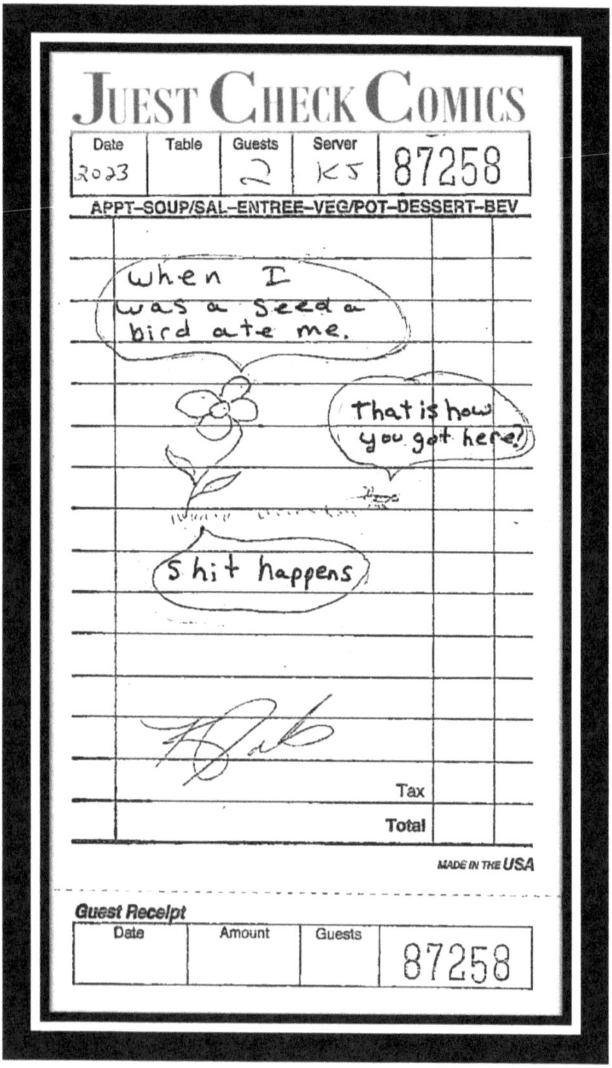
JUEST CHECK COMICS
Date 2023
Table
Guests 2
Server KS
87258
APPT–SOUP/SAL–ENTREE–VEG/POT–DESSERT–BEV
when I was a seed a bird ate me.
That is how you got here?
Shit happens
Tax
Total
MADE IN THE USA
Guest Receipt
Date
Amount
Guests
87258

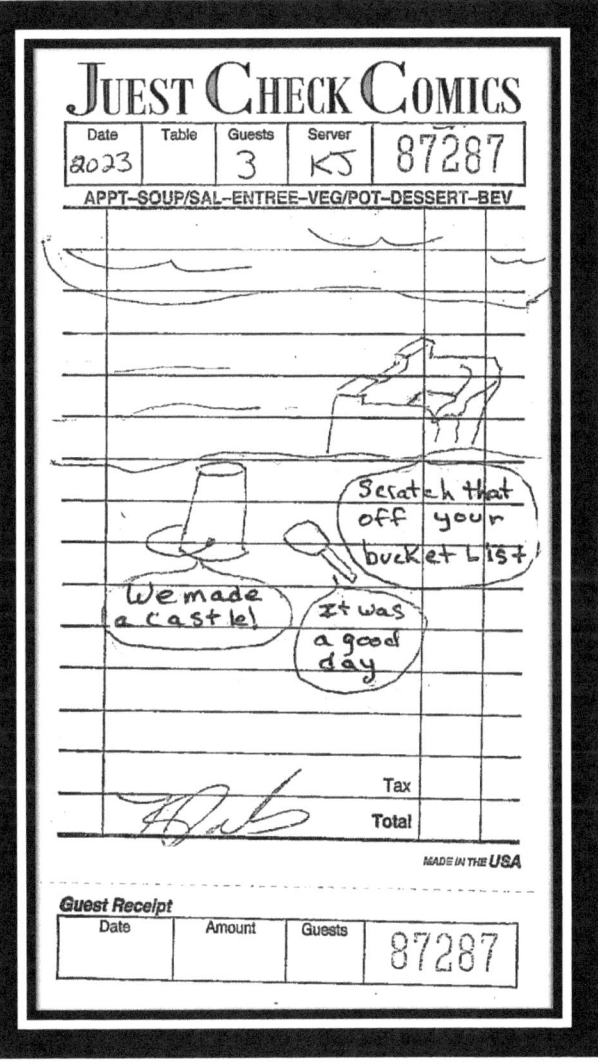

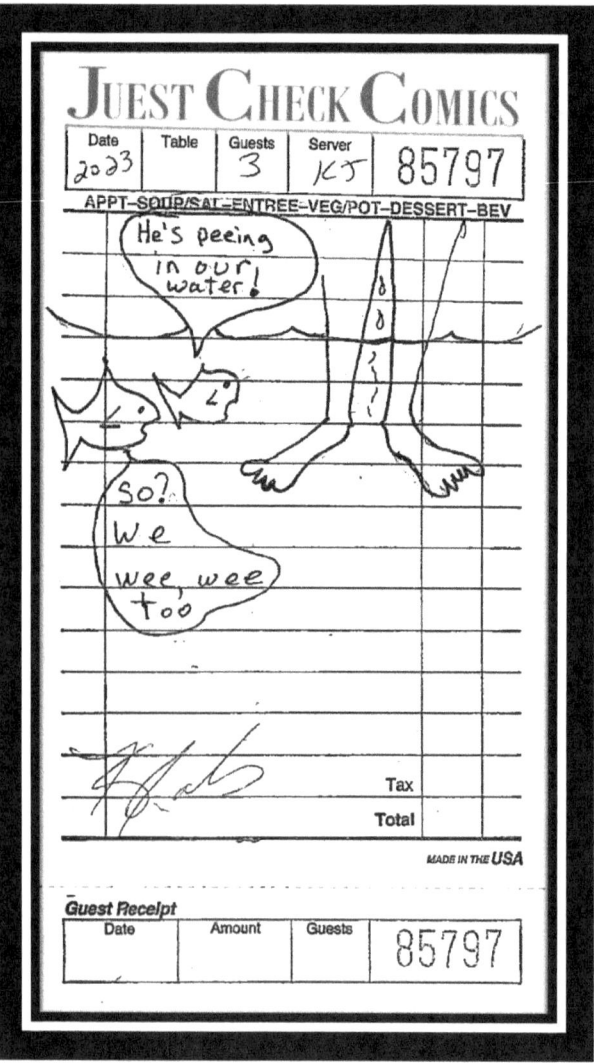

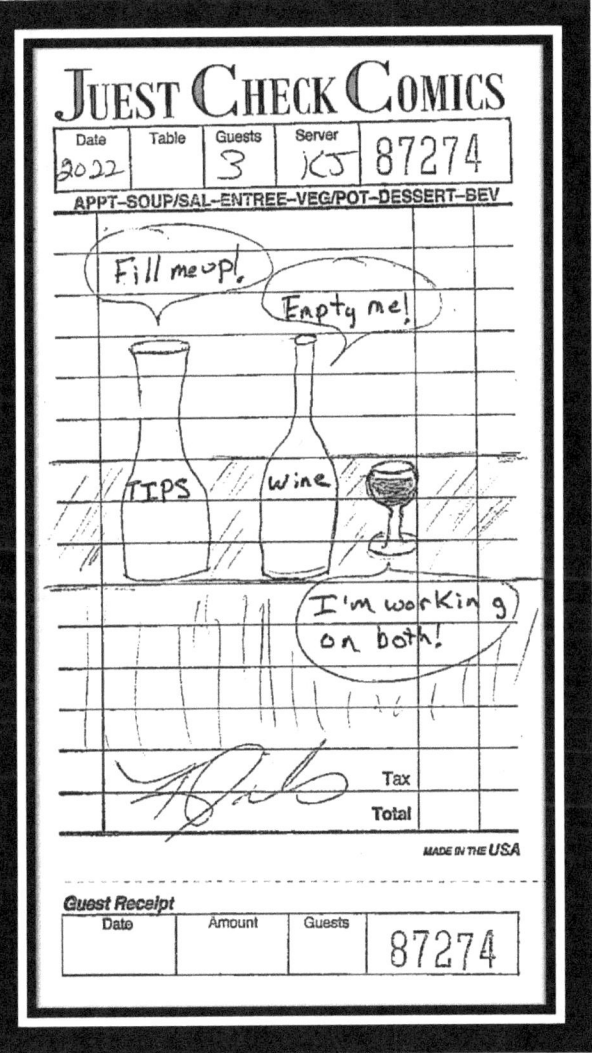

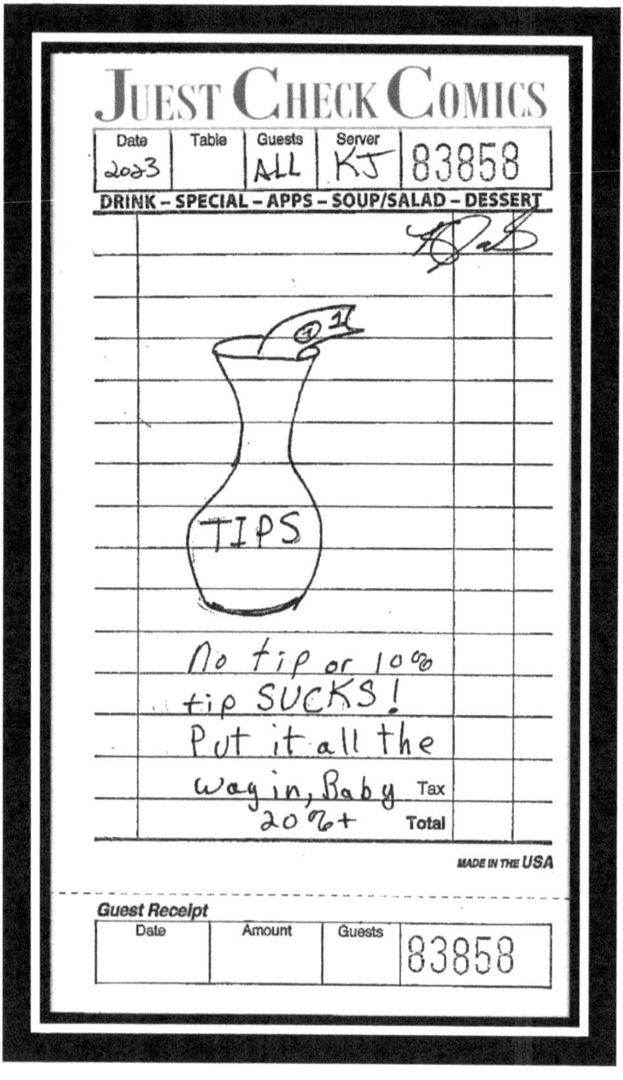
JUEST CHECK COMICS
Date 2023
Table
Guests ALL
Server KJ
83858
DRINK – SPECIAL – APPS – SOUP/SALAD – DESSERT
TIPS
No tip or 10% tip SUCKS! Put it all the way in, Baby 20%+
Tax
Total
MADE IN THE USA
Guest Receipt
Date
Amount
Guests
83858

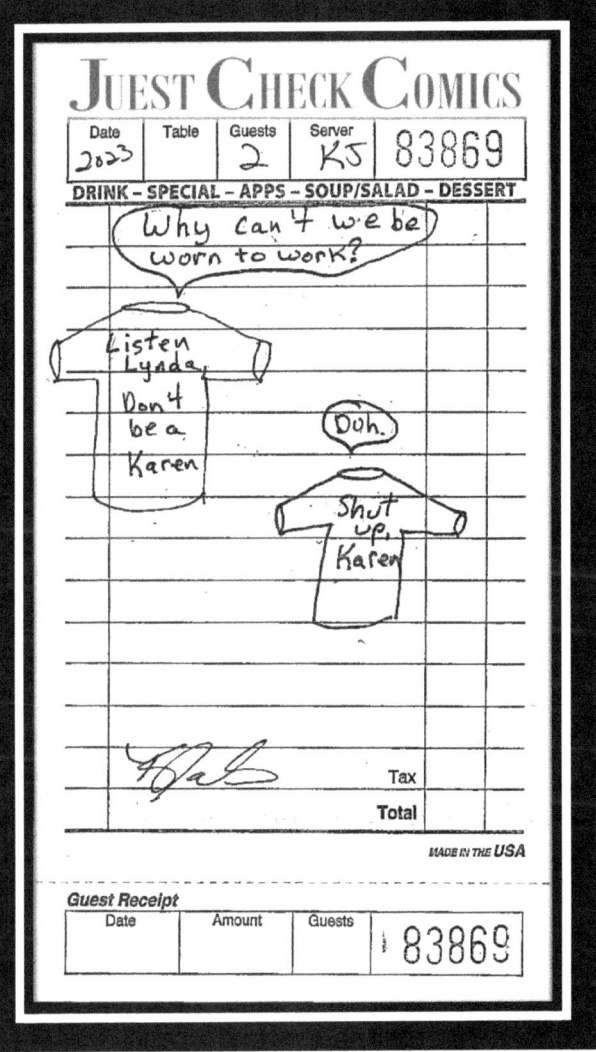

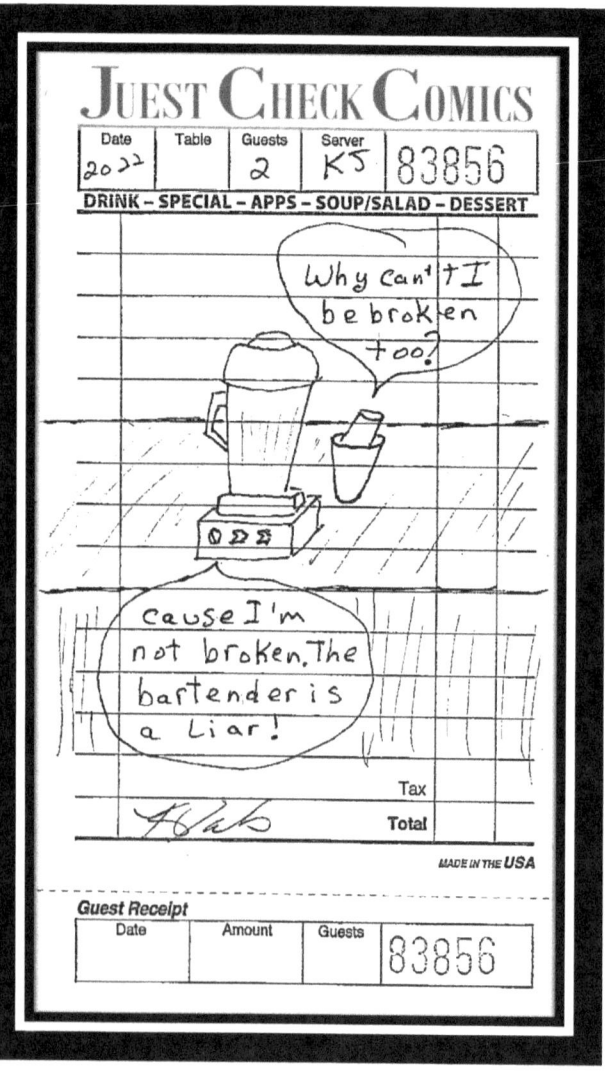

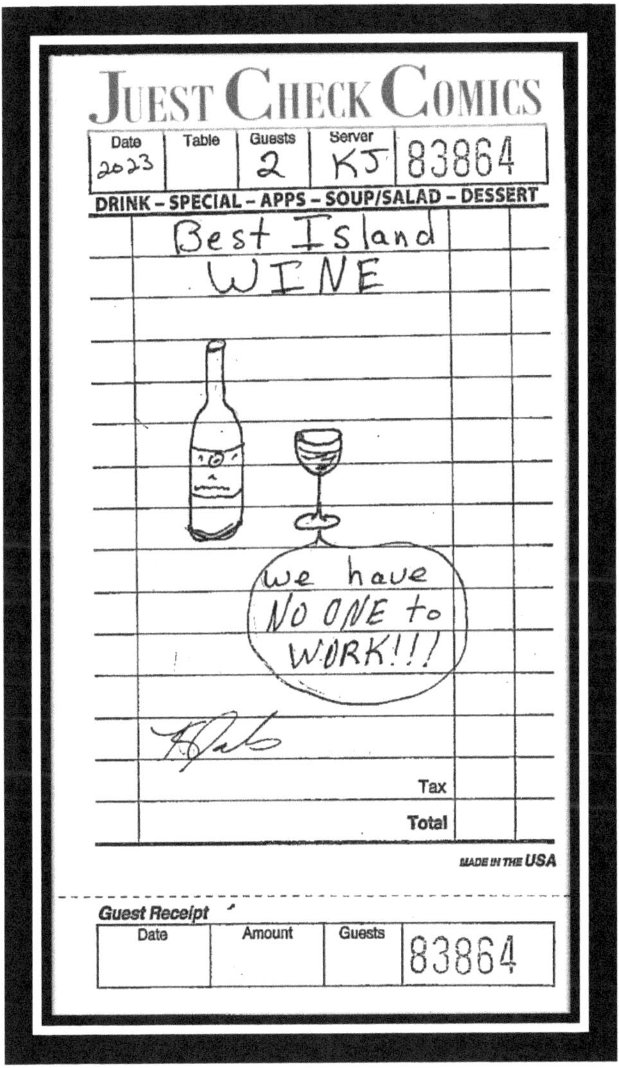
JUEST CHECK COMICS
Date
2023
Table
Guests
2
Server
KJ
83864
DRINK – SPECIAL – APPS – SOUP/SALAD – DESSERT
Best Island
WINE
we have
NO ONE to
WORK!!!
Tax
Total
MADE IN THE USA
Guest Receipt
Date
Amount
Guests
83864

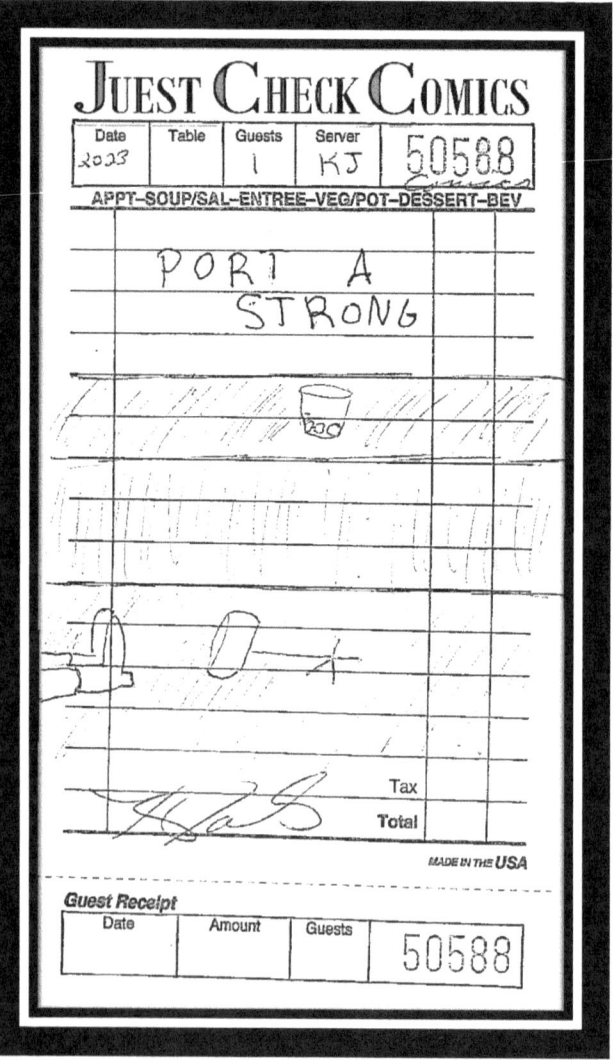

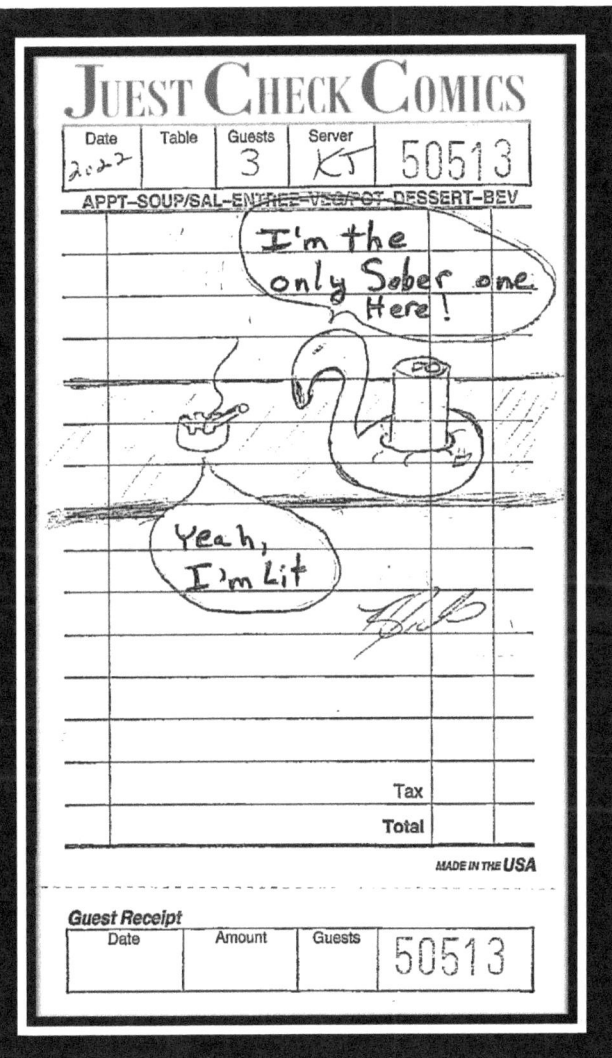

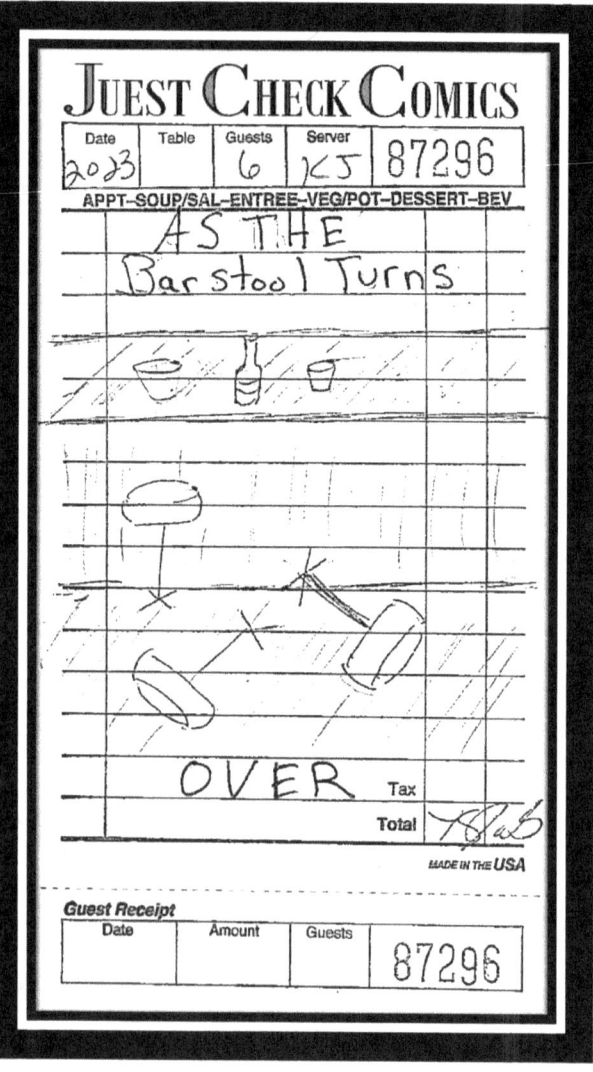

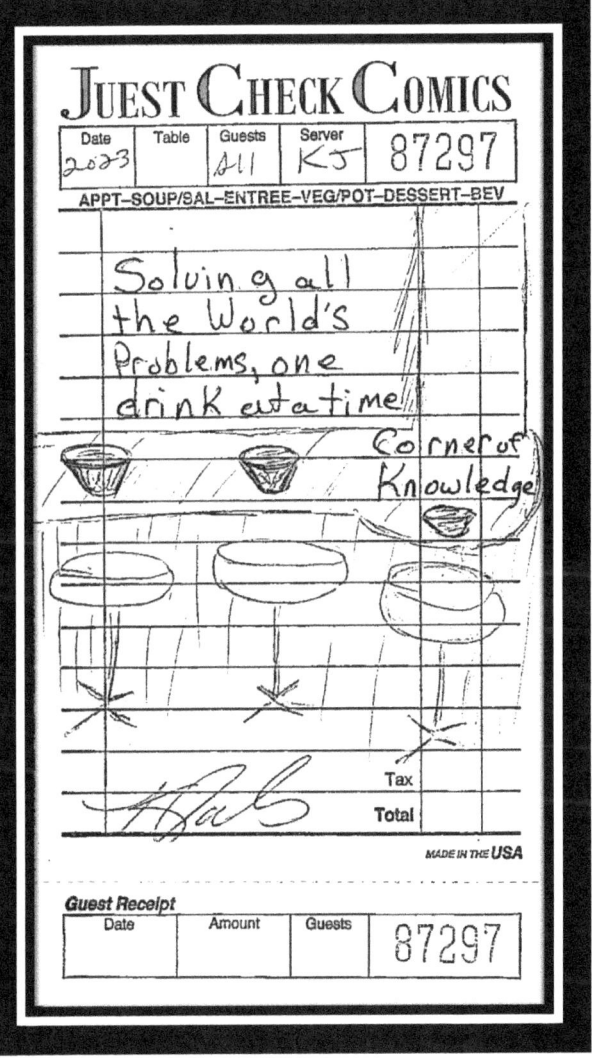

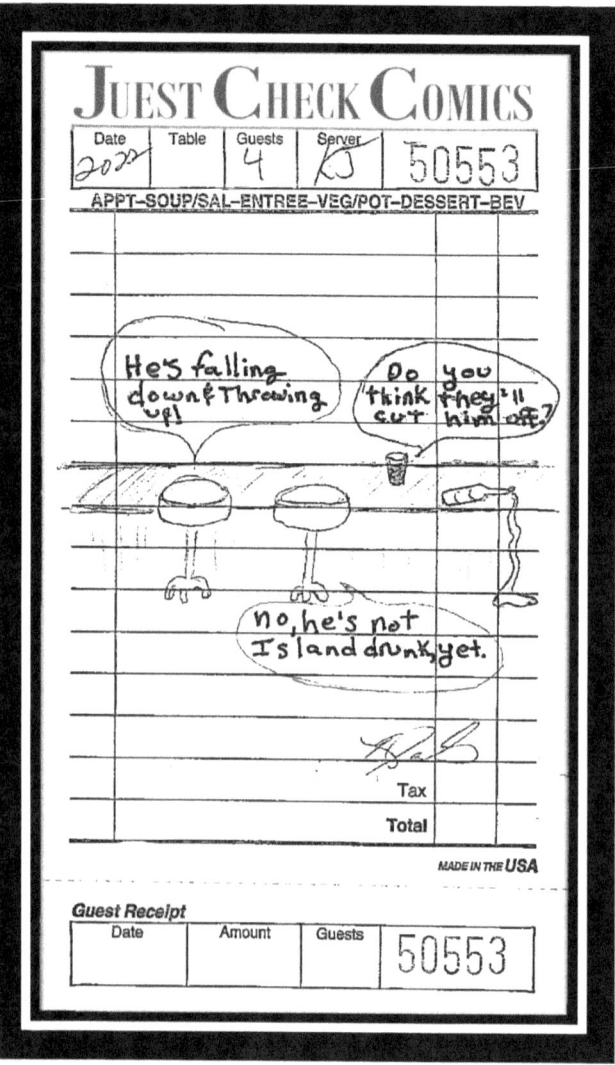

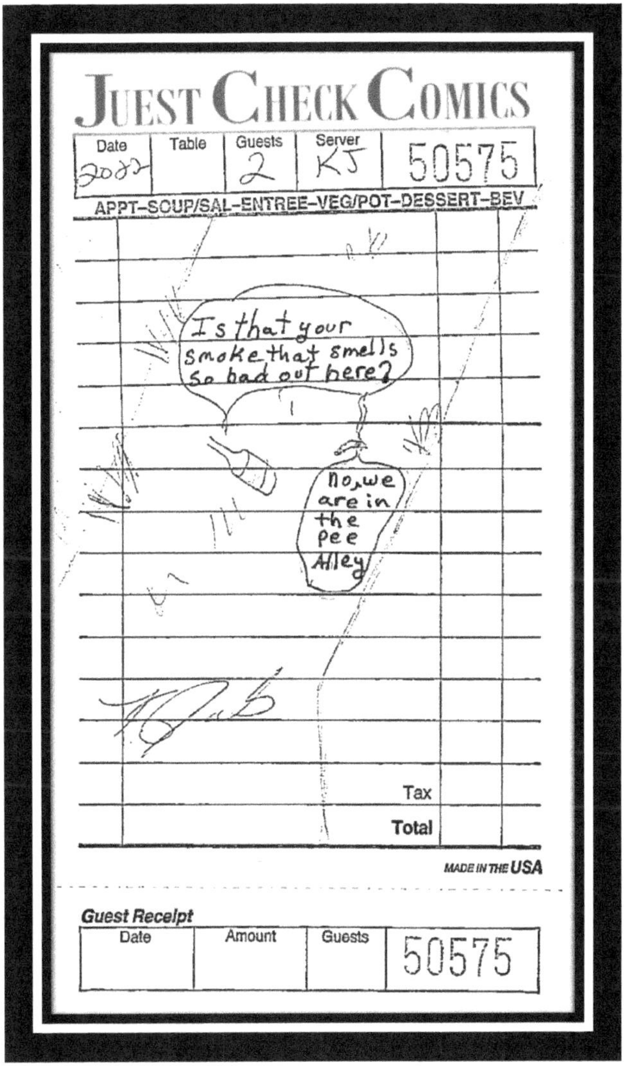
JUEST CHECK COMICS
Date Table Guests Server 50575
2022 2 KJ
APPT–SOUP/SAL–ENTREE–VEG/POT–DESSERT–BEV
Is that your smoke that smells so bad out here?
no, we are in the pee Alley
Tax
Total
MADE IN THE USA
Guest Receipt
Date Amount Guests 50575

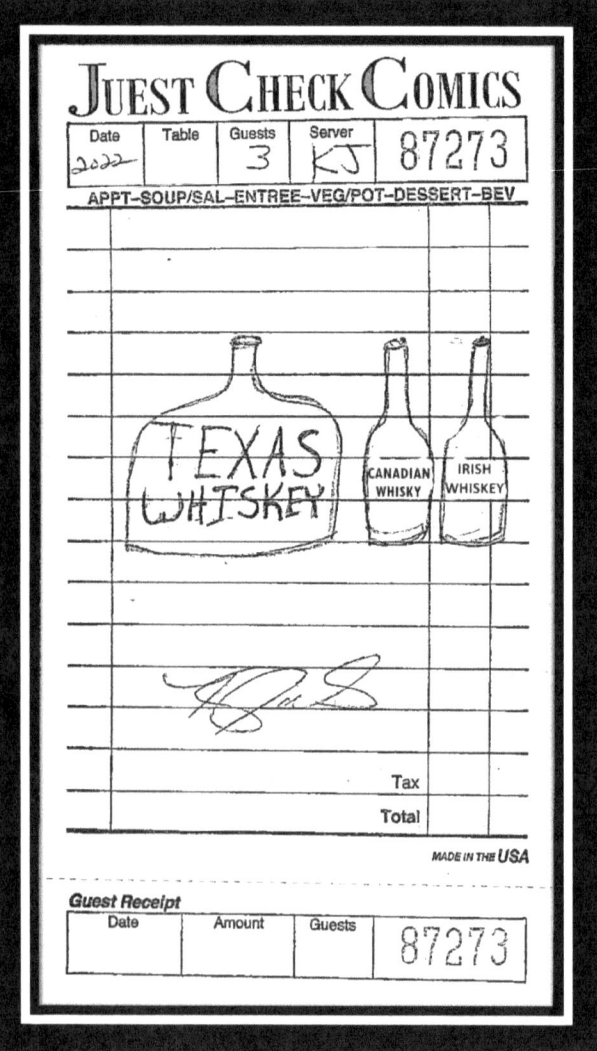

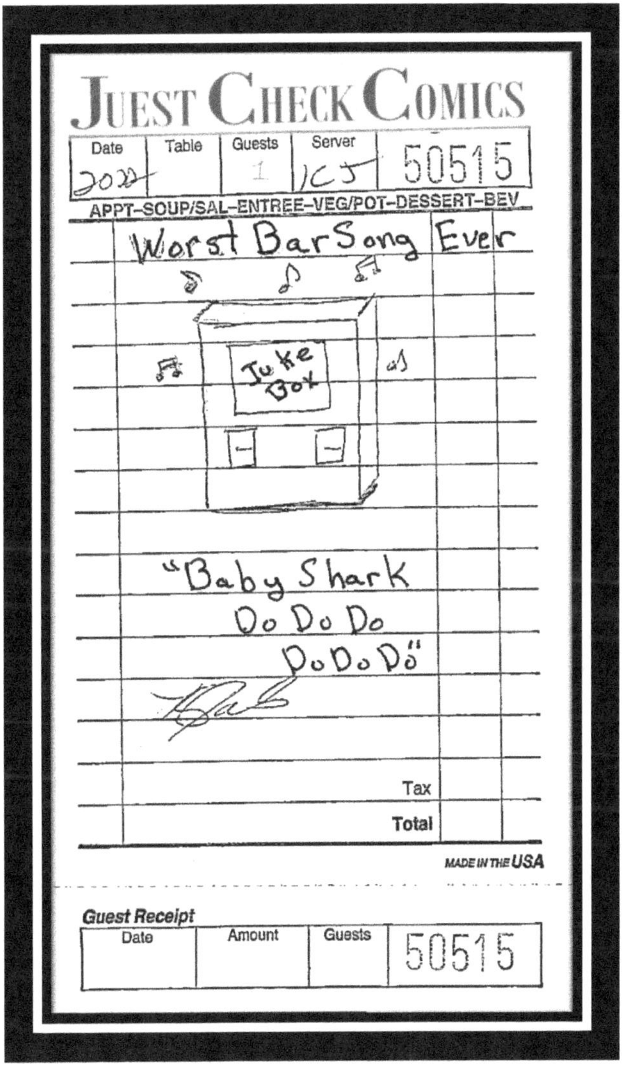
JUEST CHECK COMICS
Date
Table
Guests
Server
50515
1
APPT–SOUP/SAL–ENTREE–VEG/POT–DESSERT–BEV
Worst Bar Song Ever
Juke Box
“Baby Shark
Do Do Do
Do Do Do”
Tax
Total
MADE IN THE USA
Guest Receipt
Date
Amount
Guests
50515

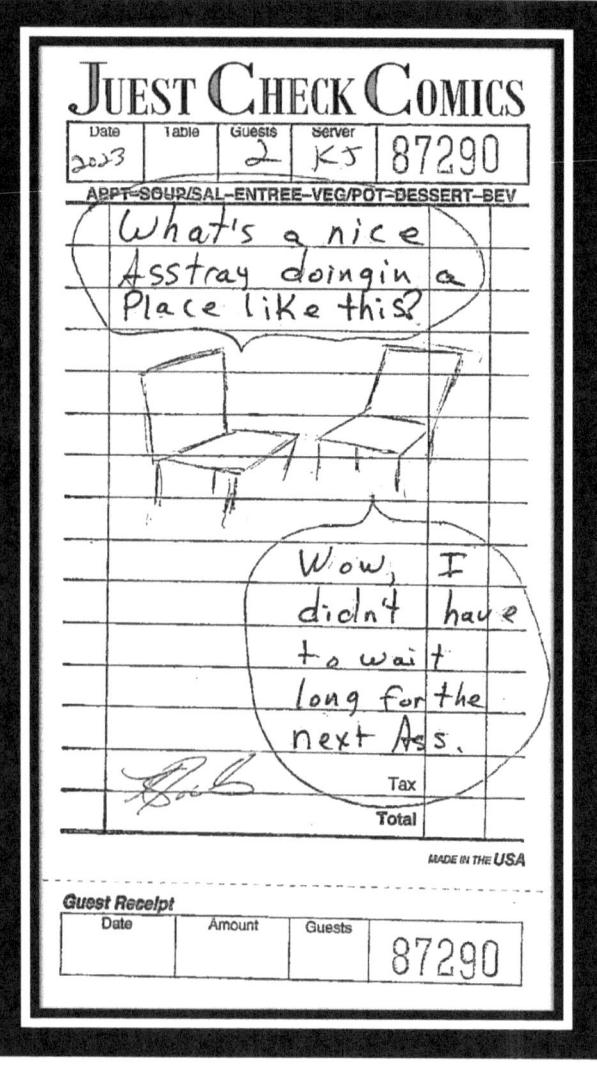

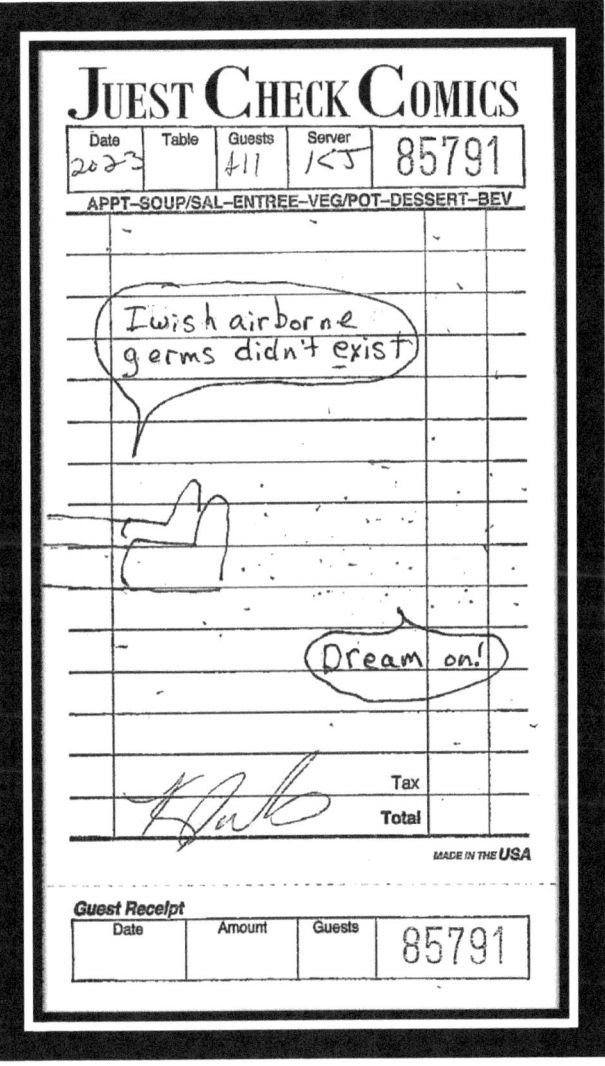

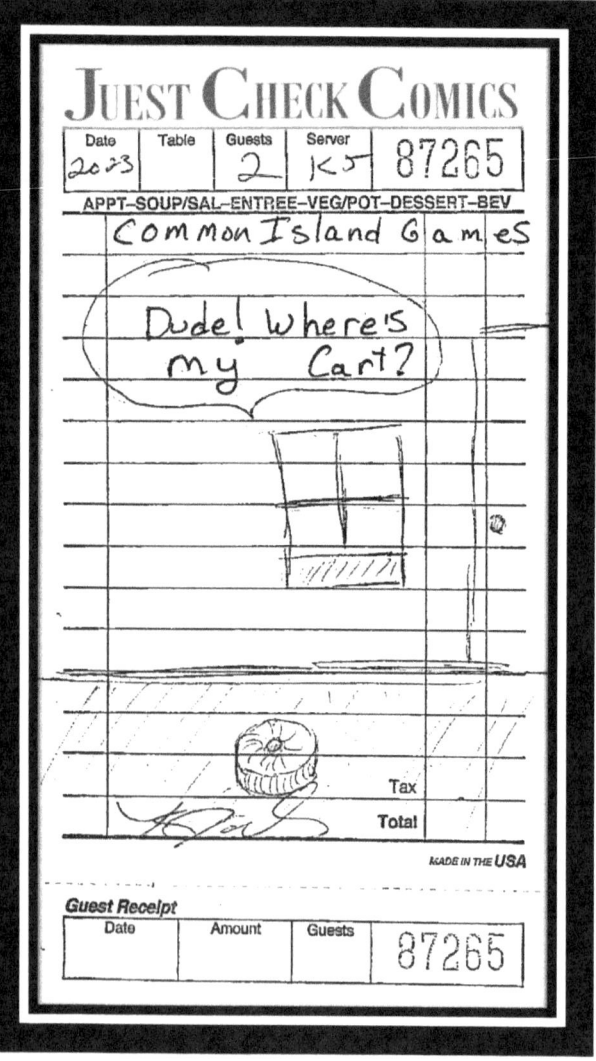

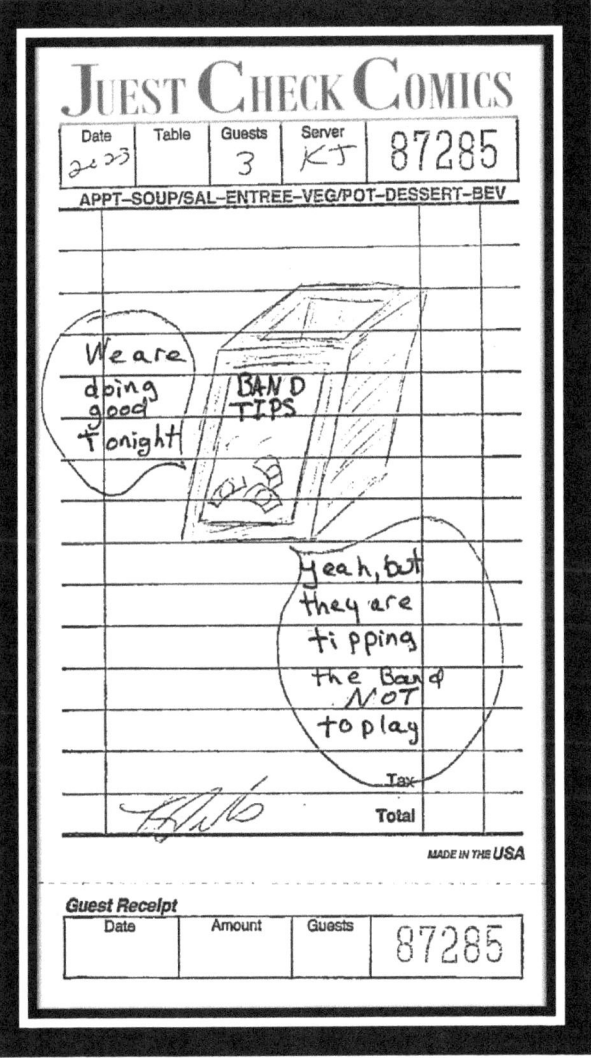

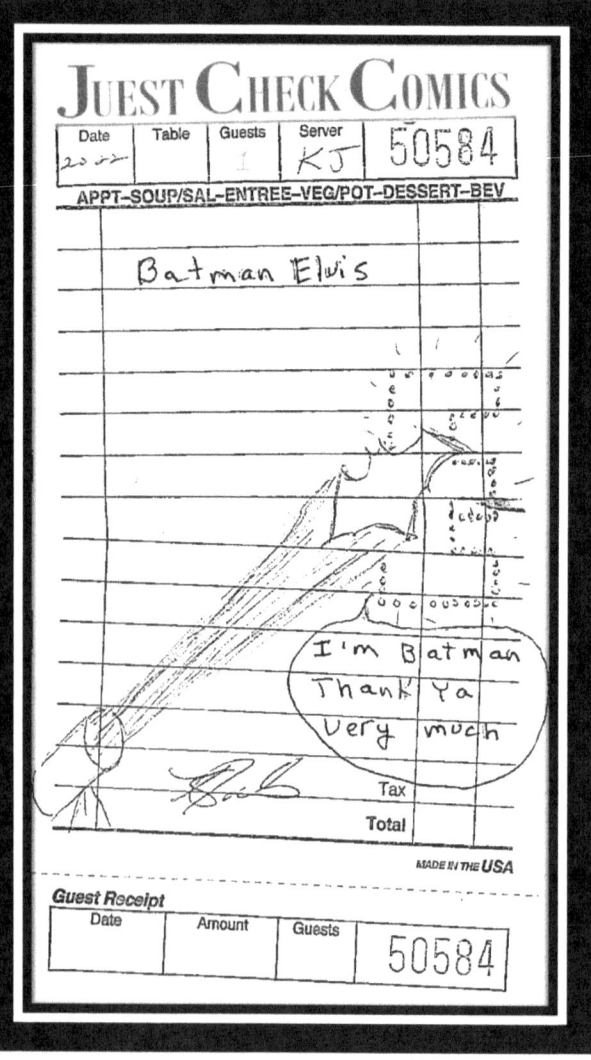

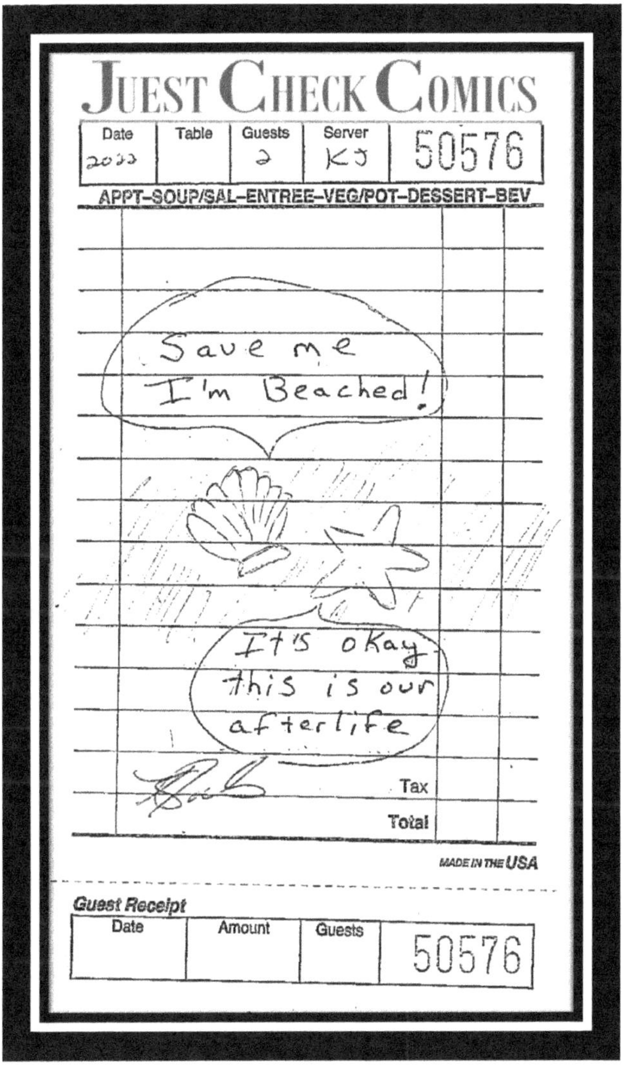
JUEST CHECK COMICS
Date
2022
Table
Guests
2
Server
KJ
50576
APPT–SOUP/SAL–ENTREE–VEG/POT–DESSERT–BEV
Save me
I'm Beached!
It's okay
this is our
afterlife
Tax
Total
MADE IN THE USA
Guest Receipt
Date
Amount
Guests
50576

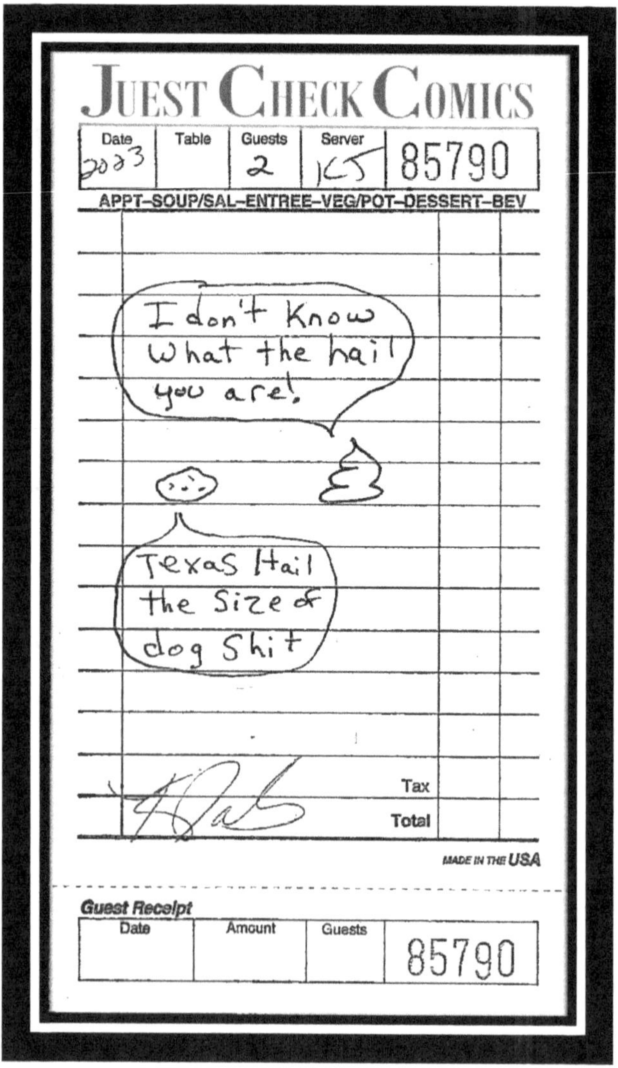
JUEST CHECK COMICS
Date 2023
Table
Guests 2
Server KS
85790
APPT–SOUP/SAL–ENTREE–VEG/POT–DESSERT–BEV
I don't Know What the hail you are!
Texas Hail the Size of dog Shit
Tax
Total
MADE IN THE USA
Guest Receipt
Date
Amount
Guests
85790

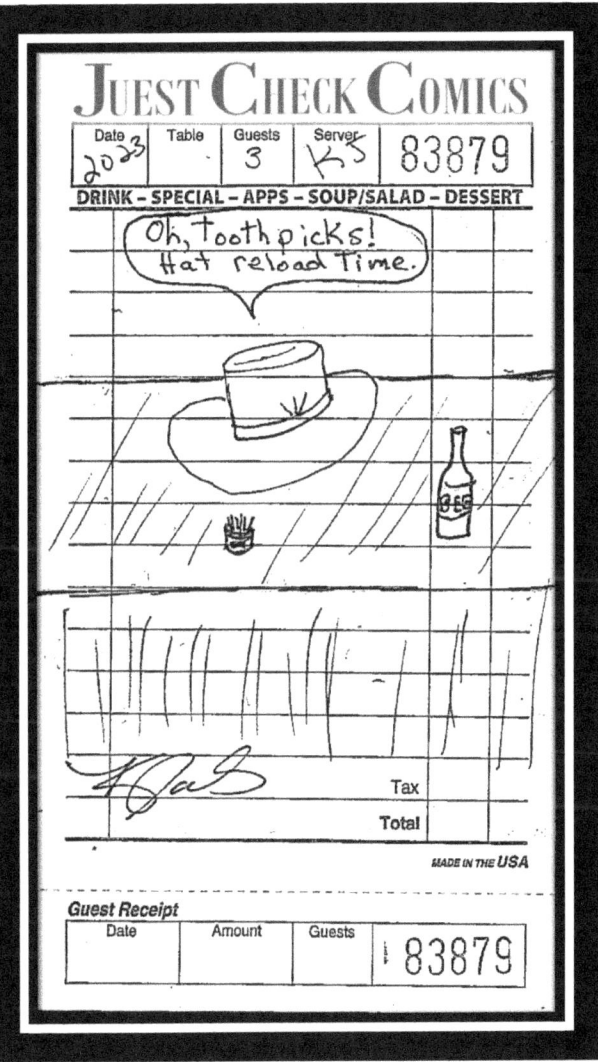

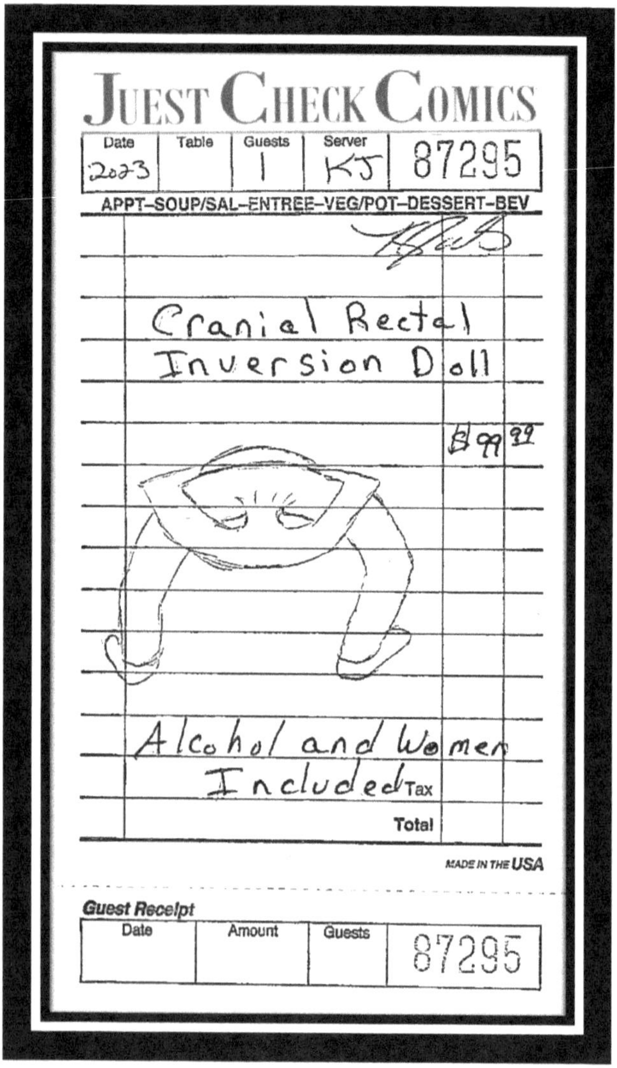
JUEST CHECK COMICS
Date
2023
Table
Guests
1
Server
KJ
87295
APPT–SOUP/SAL–ENTREE–VEG/POT–DESSERT–BEV
Cranial Rectal
Inversion Doll
$99.99
Alcohol and Women
Included
Tax
Total
MADE IN THE USA
Guest Receipt
Date
Amount
Guests
87295

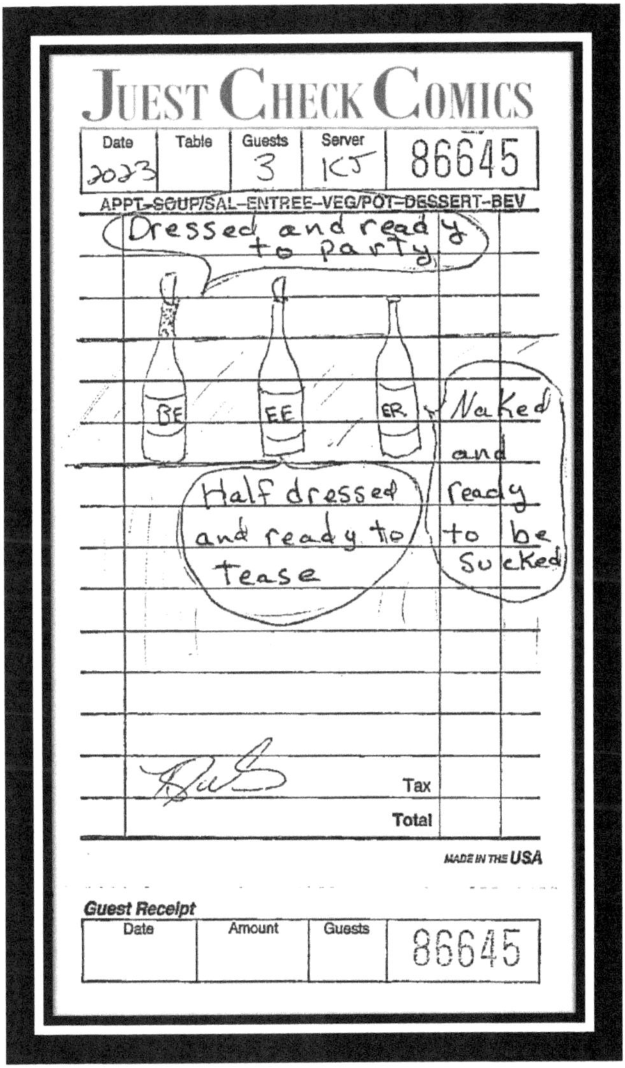
JUEST CHECK COMICS
Date 2023
Table
Guests 3
Server KJ
86645
APPT–SOUP/SAL–ENTREE–VEG/POT–DESSERT–BEV
Dressed and ready to party
BE
EE
ER
Naked and ready to be sucked
Half dressed and ready to tease
Tax
Total
MADE IN THE USA
Guest Receipt
Date
Amount
Guests
86645

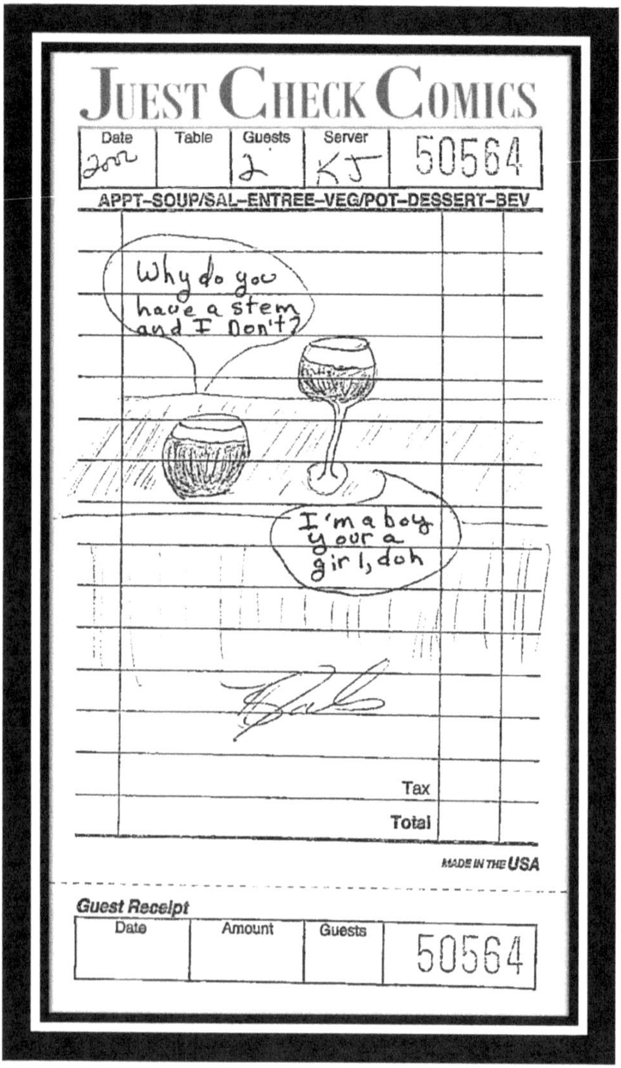
JUEST CHECK COMICS
Date
Table
Guests
Server
2
KJ
50564
APPT–SOUP/SAL–ENTREE–VEG/POT–DESSERT–BEV
Why do you have a stem and I Don't?
I'm a boy your a girl, doh
Tax
Total
MADE IN THE USA
Guest Receipt
Date
Amount
Guests
50564

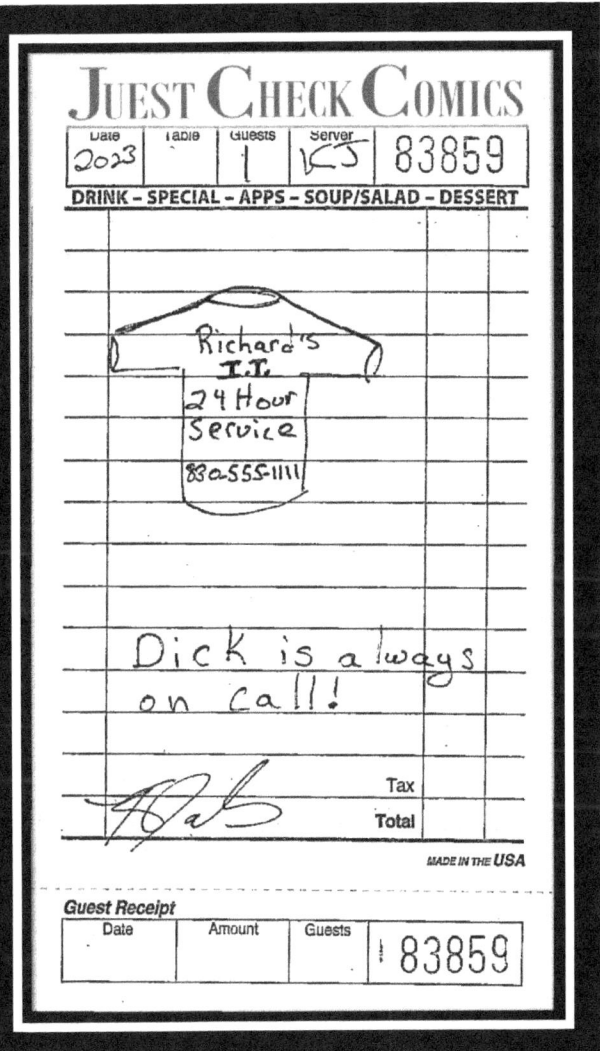

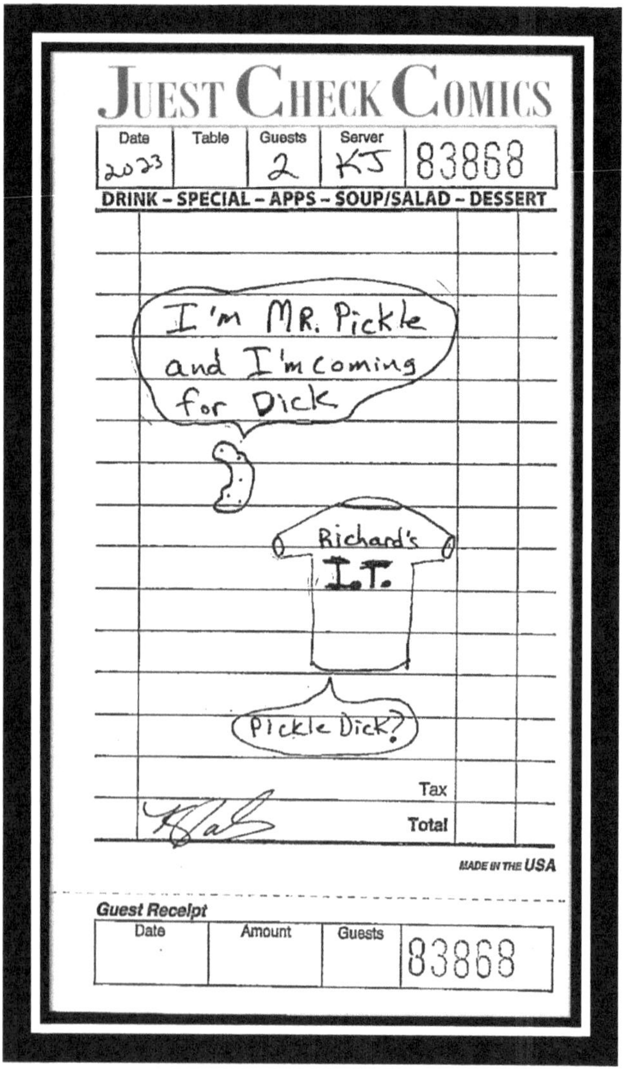
JUEST CHECK COMICS
Date
2023
Table
Guests
2
Server
KJ
83868
DRINK – SPECIAL – APPS – SOUP/SALAD – DESSERT
I'm MR. Pickle and I'm coming for Dick
Richard's I.T.
Pickle Dick?
Tax
Total
MADE IN THE USA
Guest Receipt
Date
Amount
Guests
83868

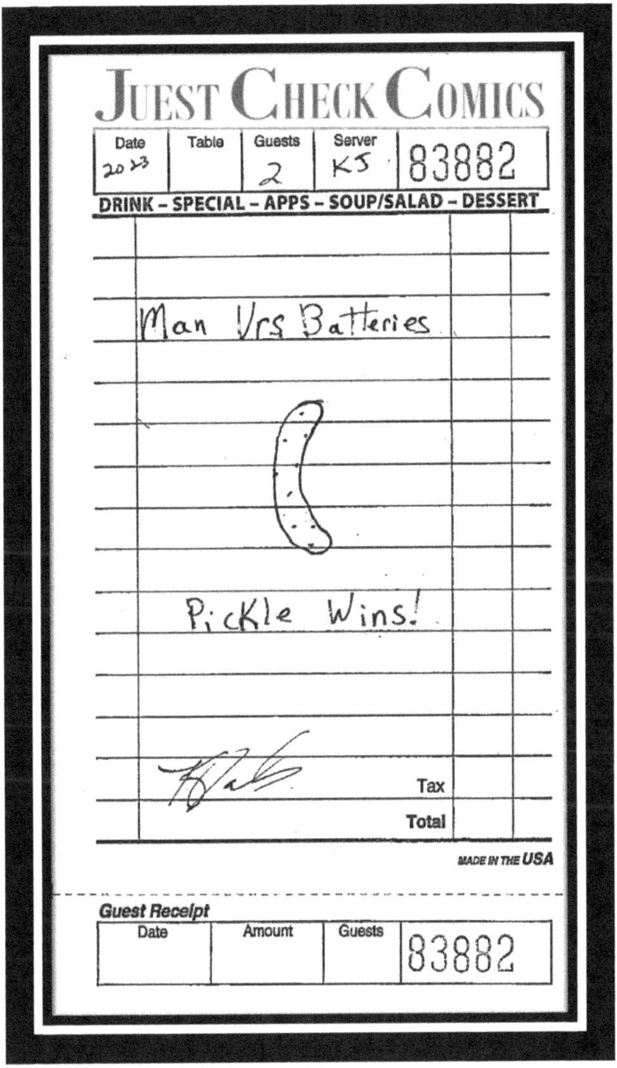
JUEST CHECK COMICS
Date
2023
Table
Guests
2
Server
KS
83882
DRINK – SPECIAL – APPS – SOUP/SALAD – DESSERT
Man Vrs Batteries
Pickle Wins!
Tax
Total
MADE IN THE USA
Guest Receipt
Date
Amount
Guests
83882

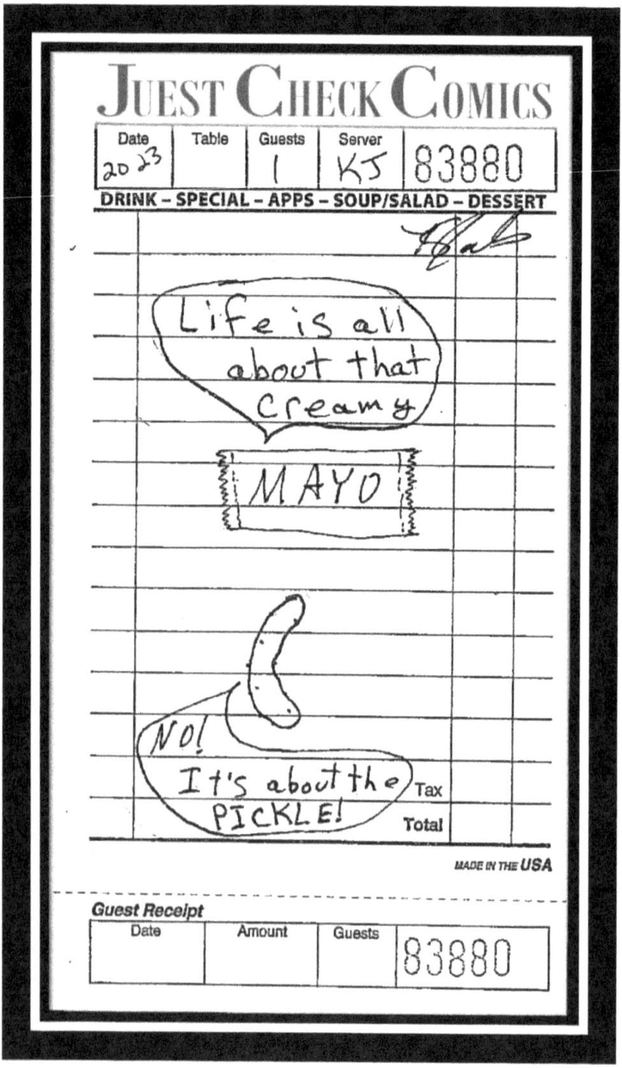
JUEST CHECK COMICS
Date 2023
Table
Guests 1
Server KJ
83880
DRINK – SPECIAL – APPS – SOUP/SALAD – DESSERT
Life is all about that creamy
MAYO
NO! It's about the PICKLE!
Tax
Total
MADE IN THE USA
Guest Receipt
Date
Amount
Guests
83880

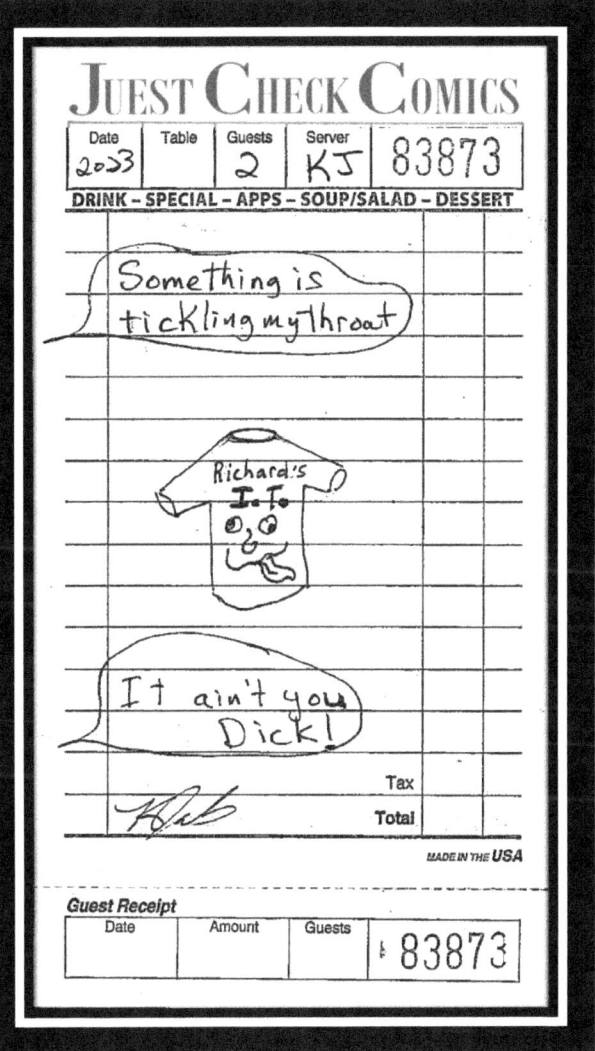

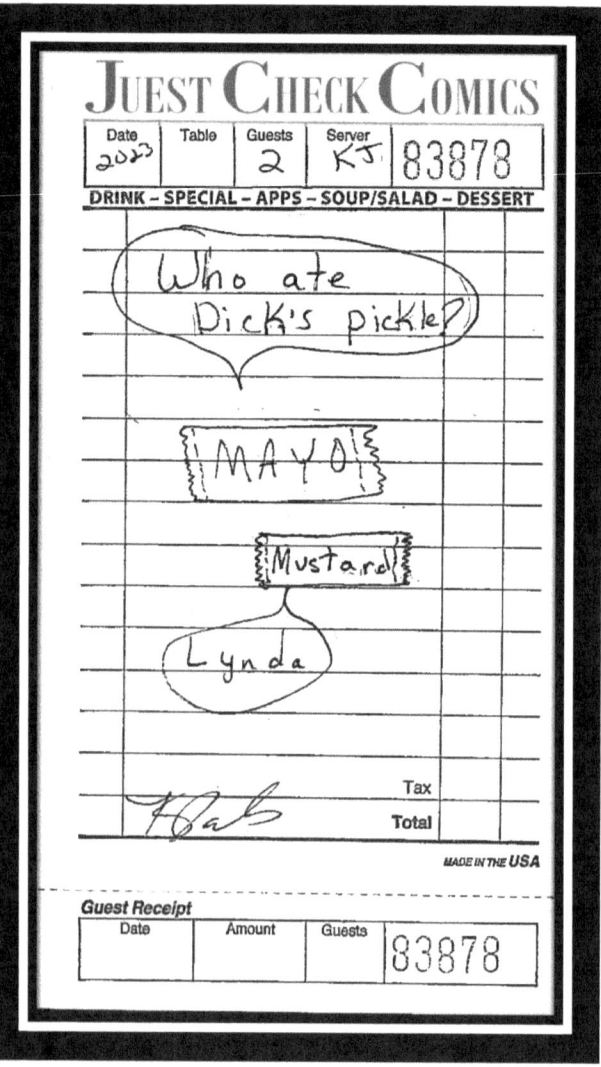

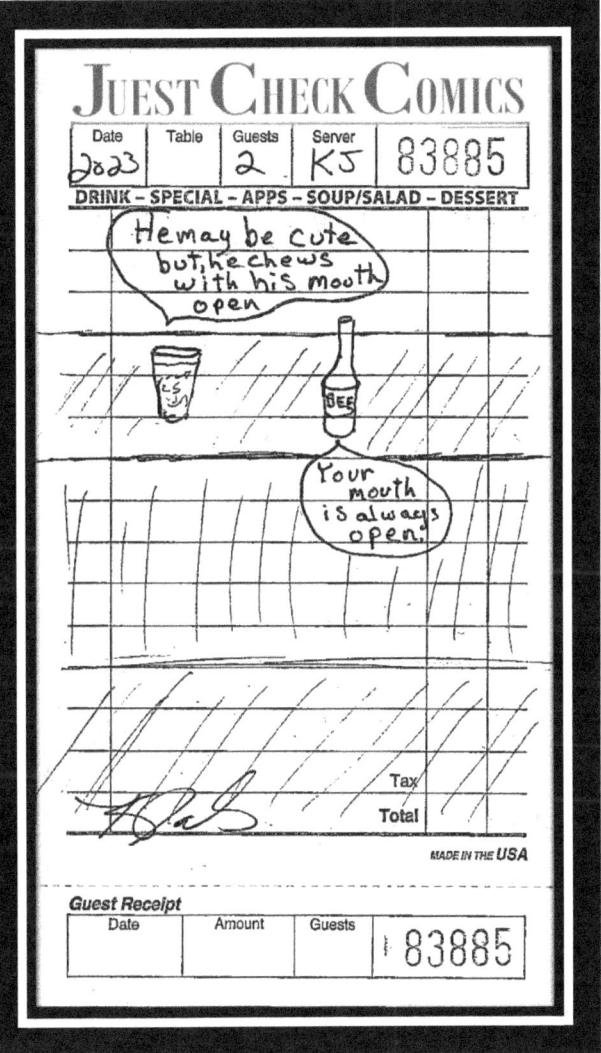

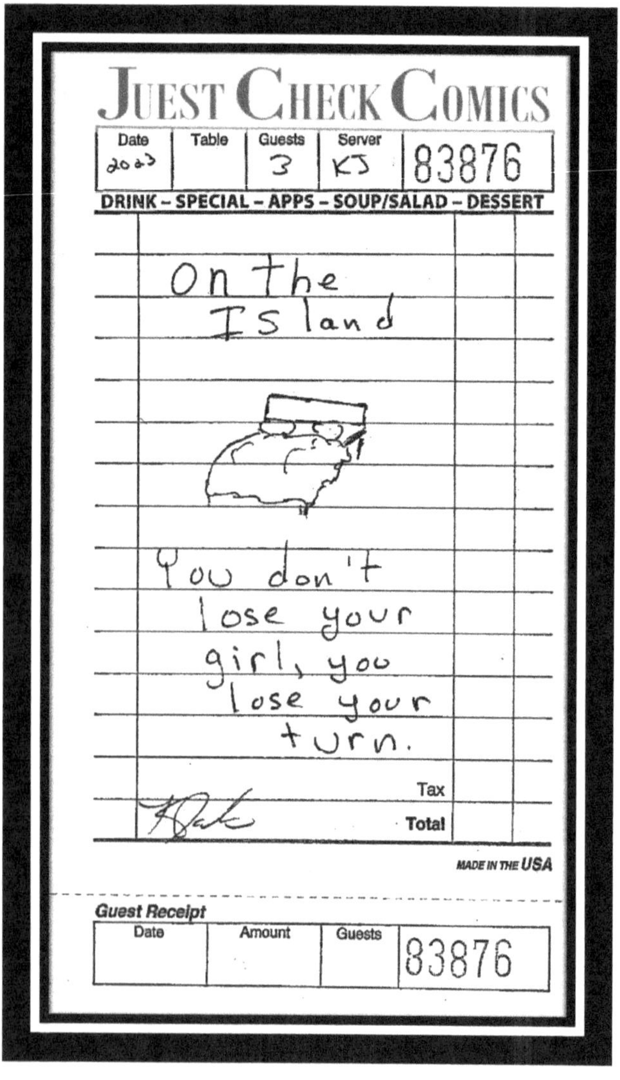
JUEST CHECK COMICS
Date
2023
Table
Guests
3
Server
KJ
83876
DRINK – SPECIAL – APPS – SOUP/SALAD – DESSERT
On the
Island
You don't
lose your
girl, you
lose your
turn.
Tax
Total
MADE IN THE USA
Guest Receipt
Date
Amount
Guests
83876

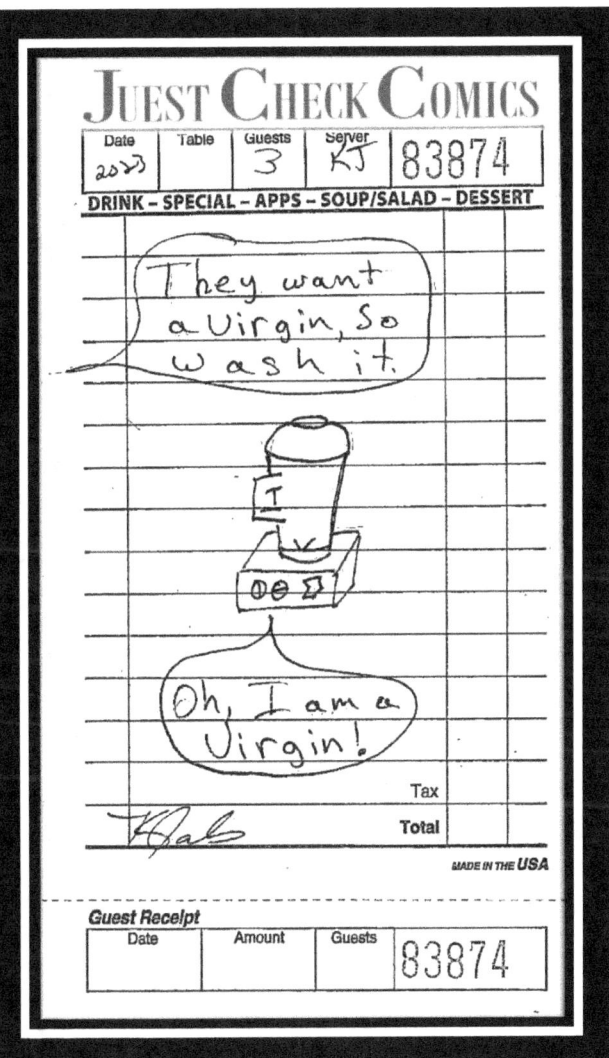

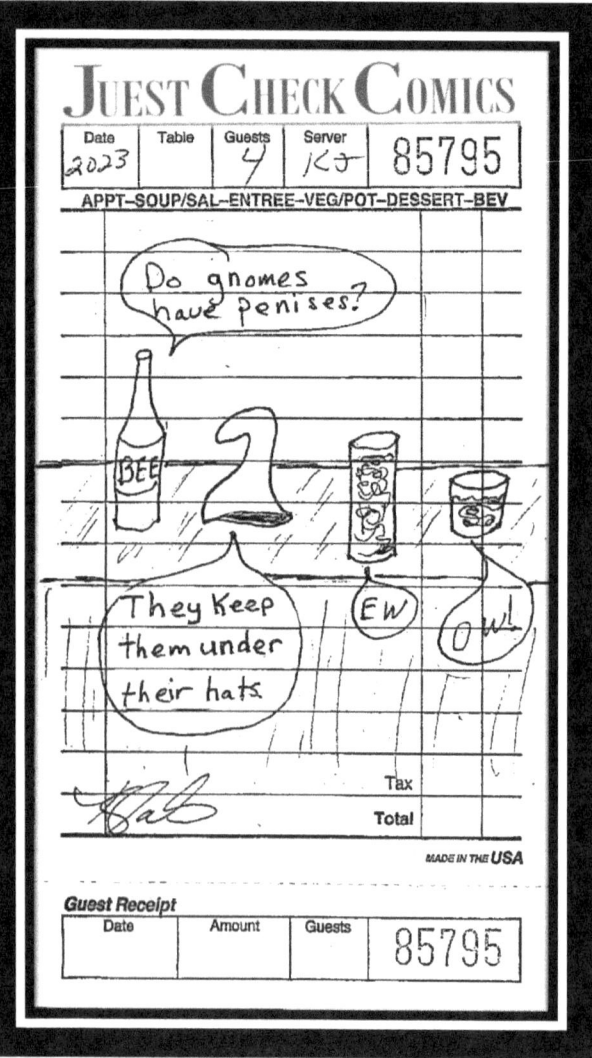

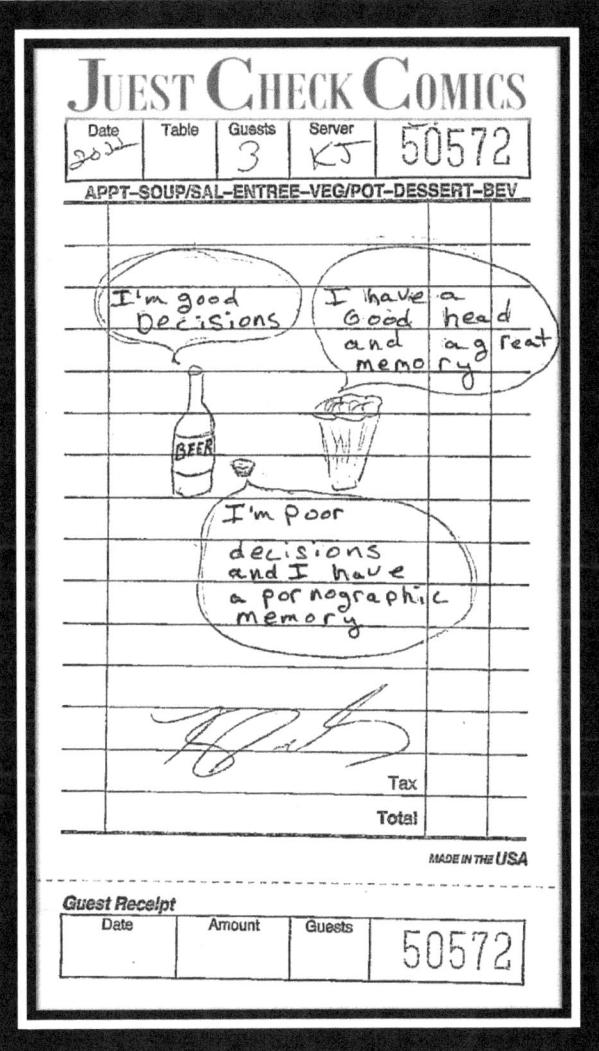

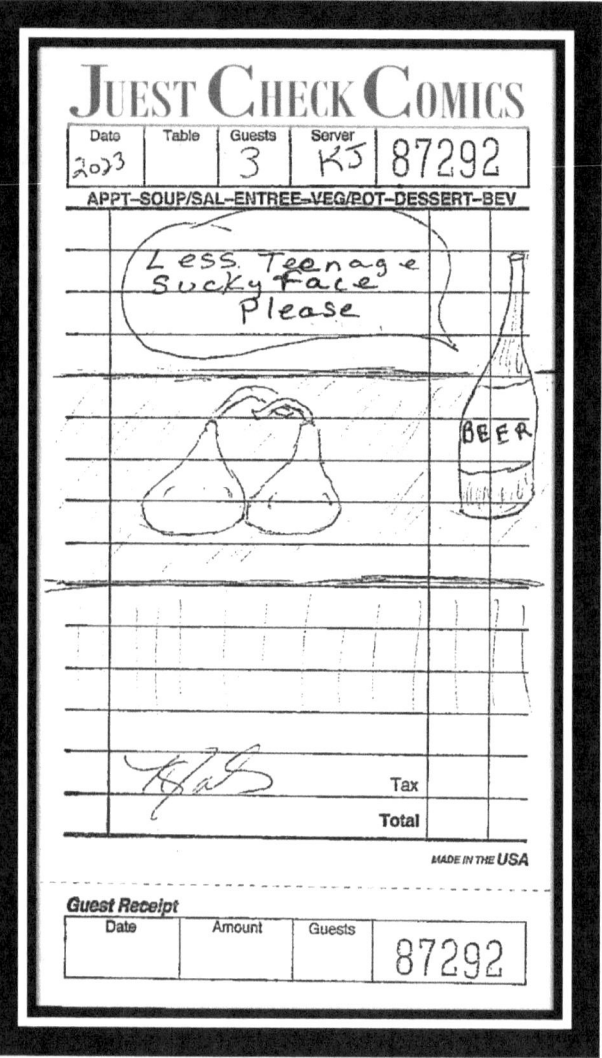

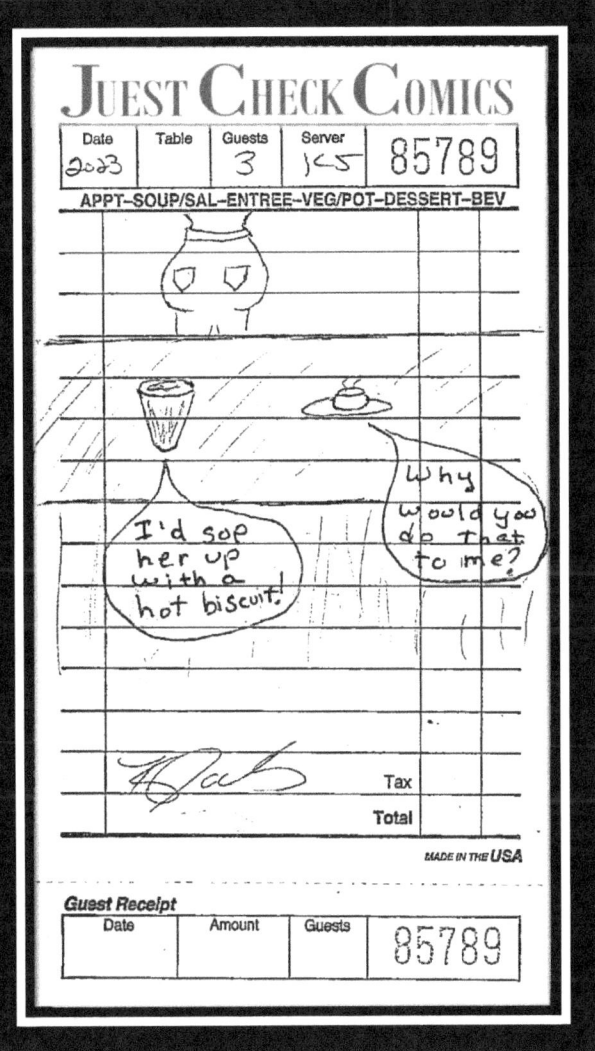

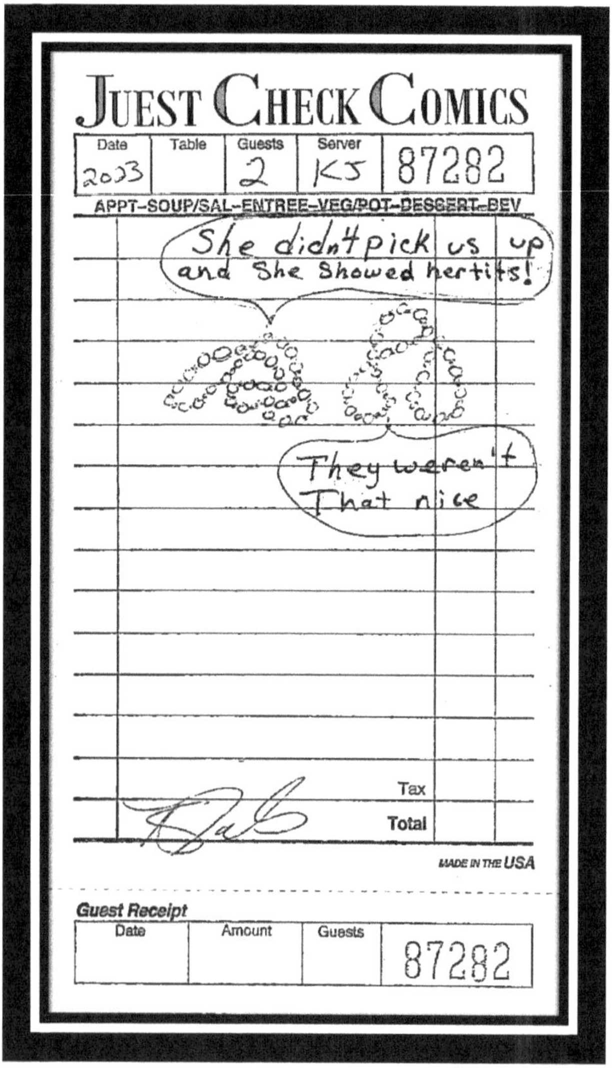
JUEST CHECK COMICS
Date
2023
Table
Guests
2
Server
KS
87282
APPT–SOUP/SAL–ENTREE–VEG/POT–DESSERT–BEV
She didn't pick us up and She showed her tits!
They weren't That nice
Tax
Total
MADE IN THE USA
Guest Receipt
Date
Amount
Guests
87282

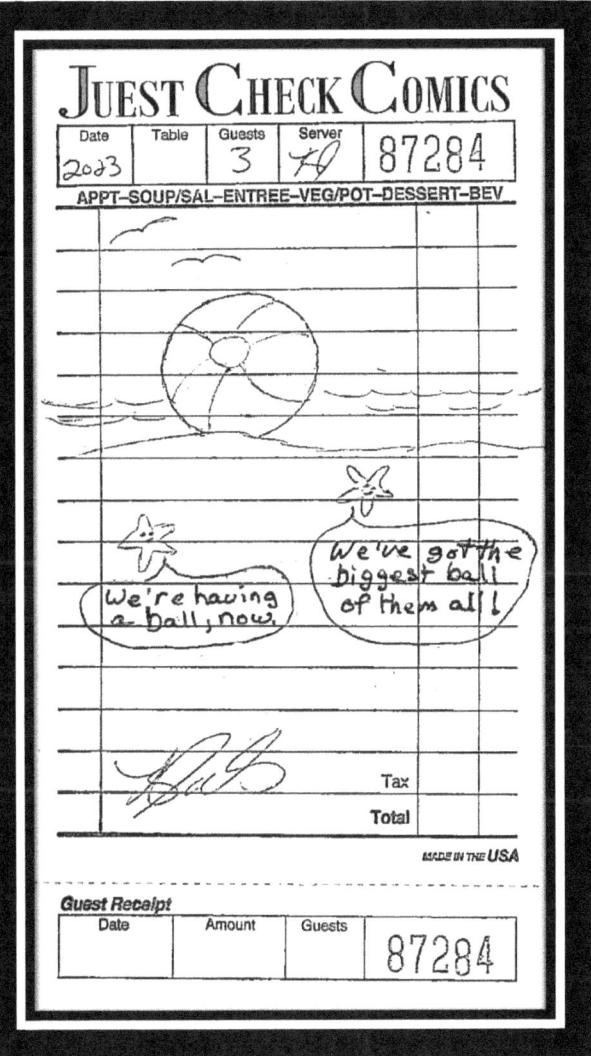

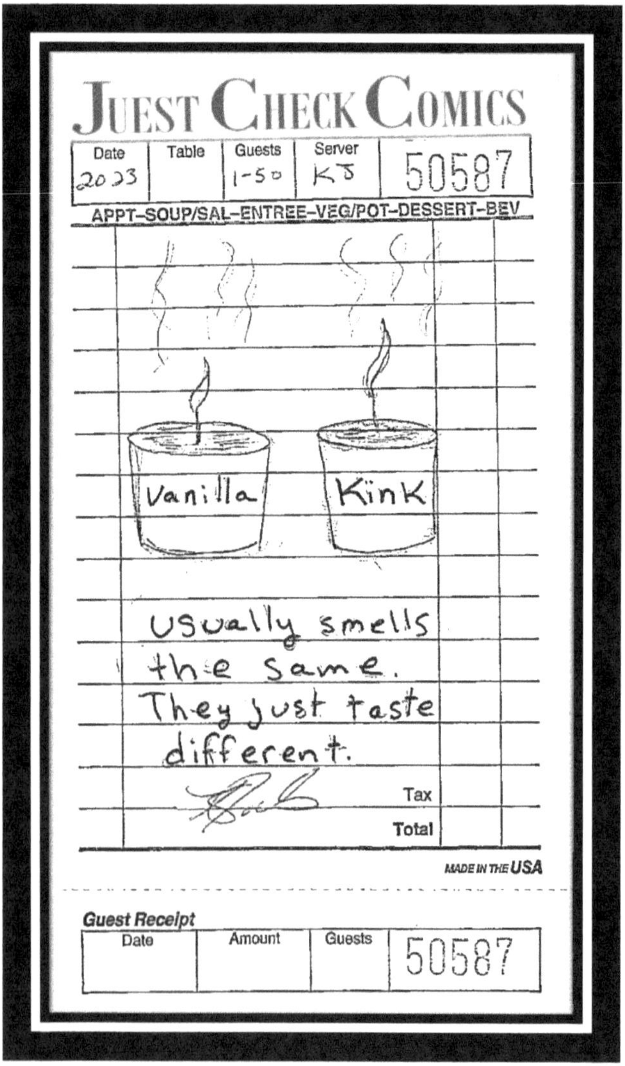
JUEST CHECK COMICS
Date
2023
Table
Guests
1-50
Server
KJ
50587
APPT–SOUP/SAL–ENTREE–VEG/POT–DESSERT–BEV
Vanilla
Kink
usually smells
the same.
They just taste
different.
Tax
Total
MADE IN THE USA
Guest Receipt
Date
Amount
Guests
50587

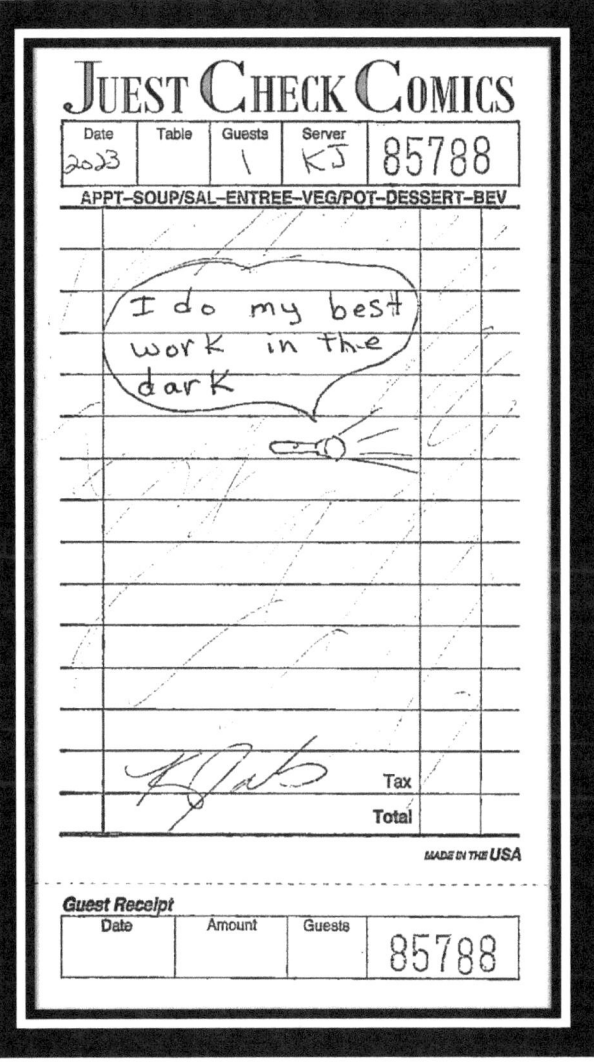

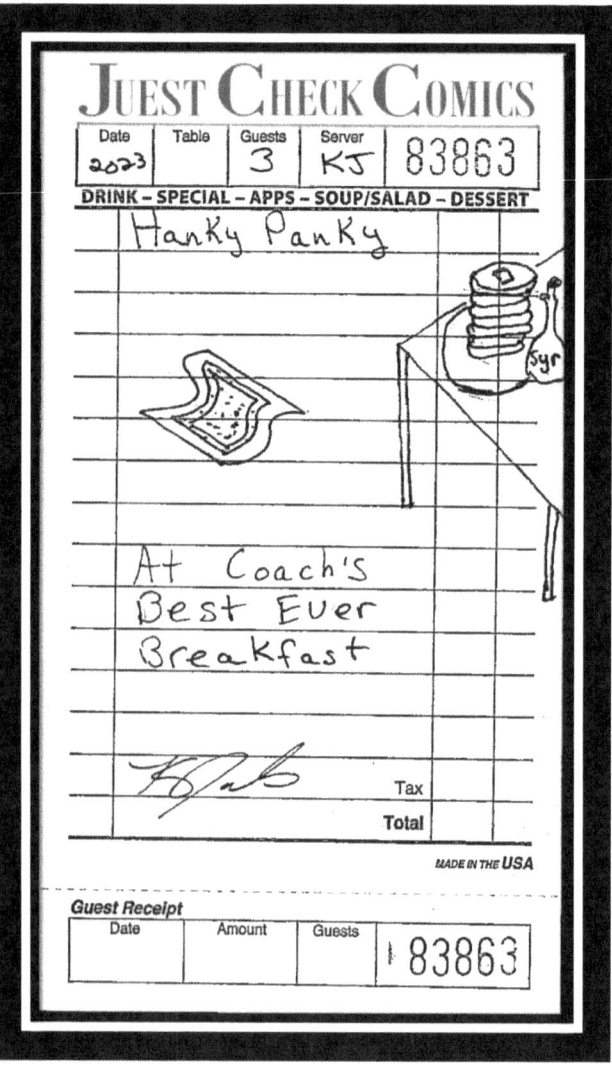

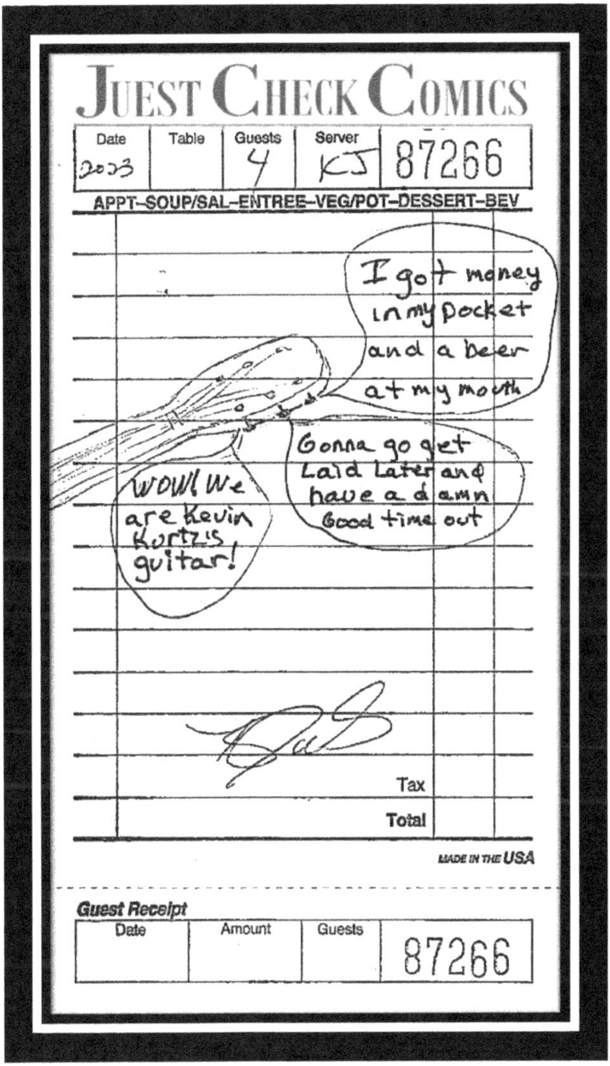
JUEST CHECK COMICS
Date 2023
Table
Guests 4
Server KJ
87266
APPT–SOUP/SAL–ENTREE–VEG/POT–DESSERT–BEV
I got money in my pocket and a beer at my mouth
Gonna go get Laid Later and have a damn Good time out
WOW! We are Kevin Kurtz's guitar!
Tax
Total
MADE IN THE USA
Guest Receipt
Date
Amount
Guests
87266

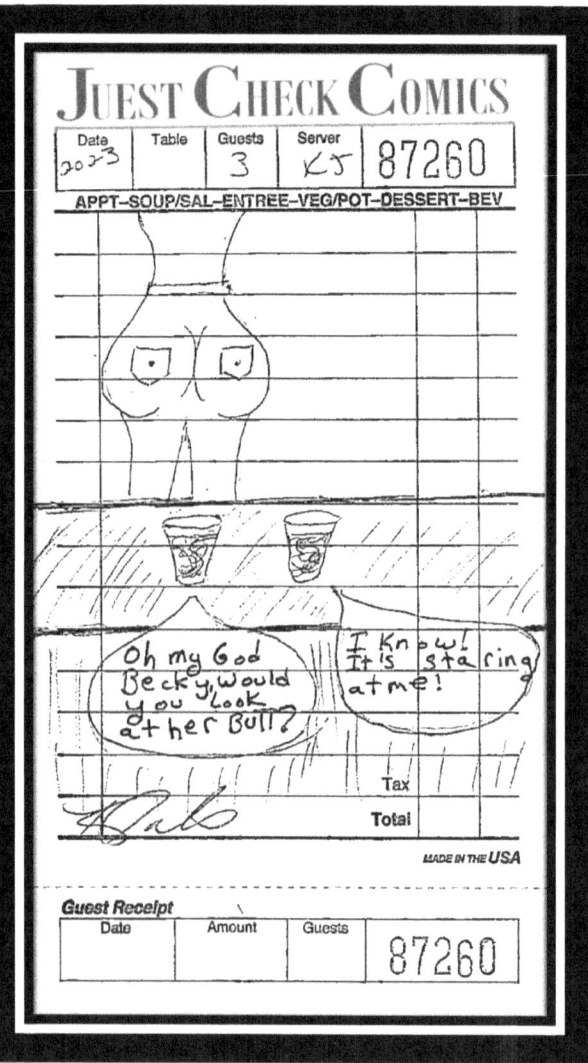

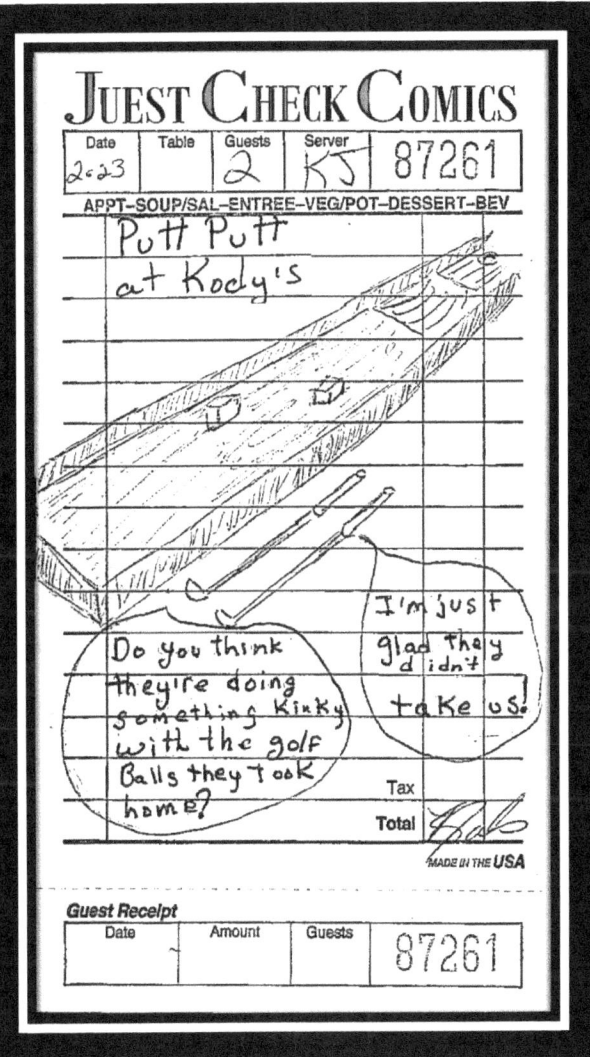

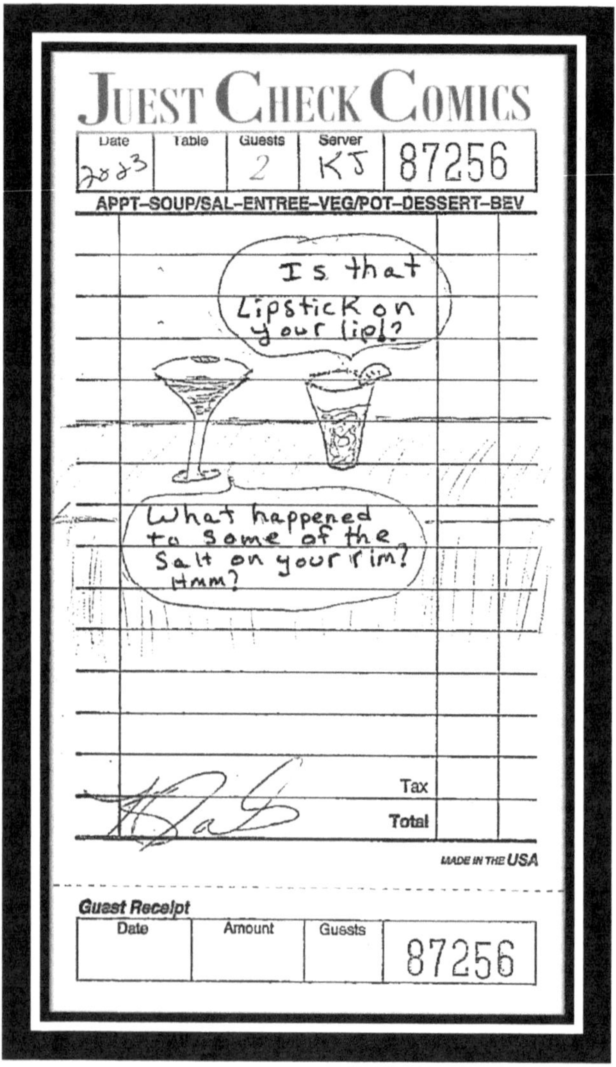
JUEST CHECK COMICS
Date 2023
Table
Guests 2
Server KJ
87256
APPT–SOUP/SAL–ENTREE–VEG/POT–DESSERT–BEV
Is that Lipstick on your lip?
What happened to some of the salt on your rim? Hmm?
Tax
Total
MADE IN THE USA
Guest Receipt
Date
Amount
Guests
87256

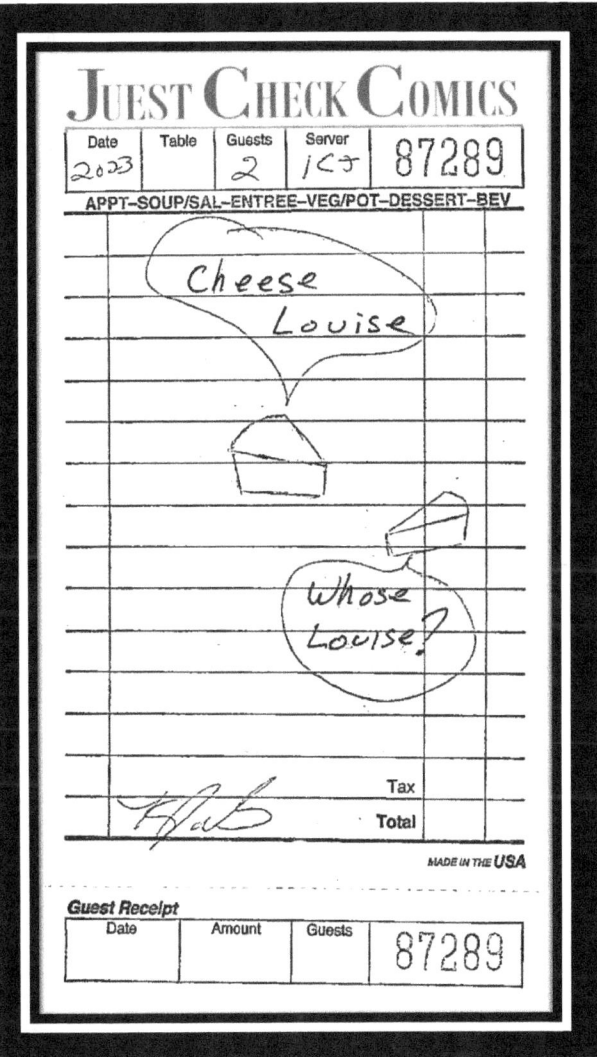

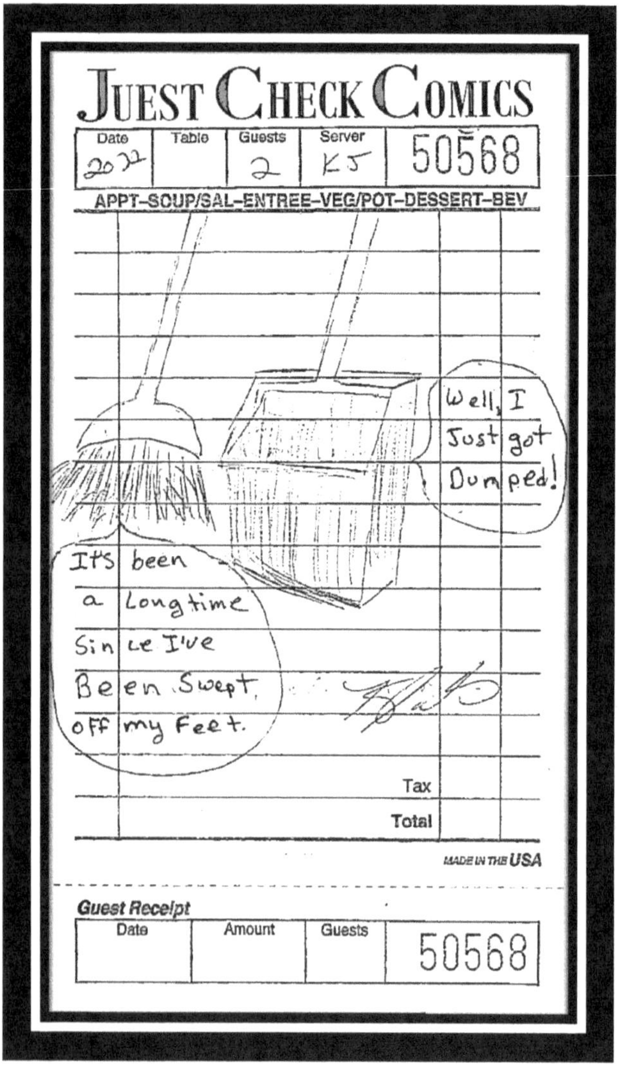
JUEST CHECK COMICS
Date 2022
Table
Guests 2
Server KJ
50568
APPT–SOUP/SAL–ENTREE–VEG/POT–DESSERT–BEV
Well, I Just got Dumped!
It's been a Long time Since I've Been Swept off my Feet.
Tax
Total
MADE IN THE USA
Guest Receipt
Date
Amount
Guests
50568

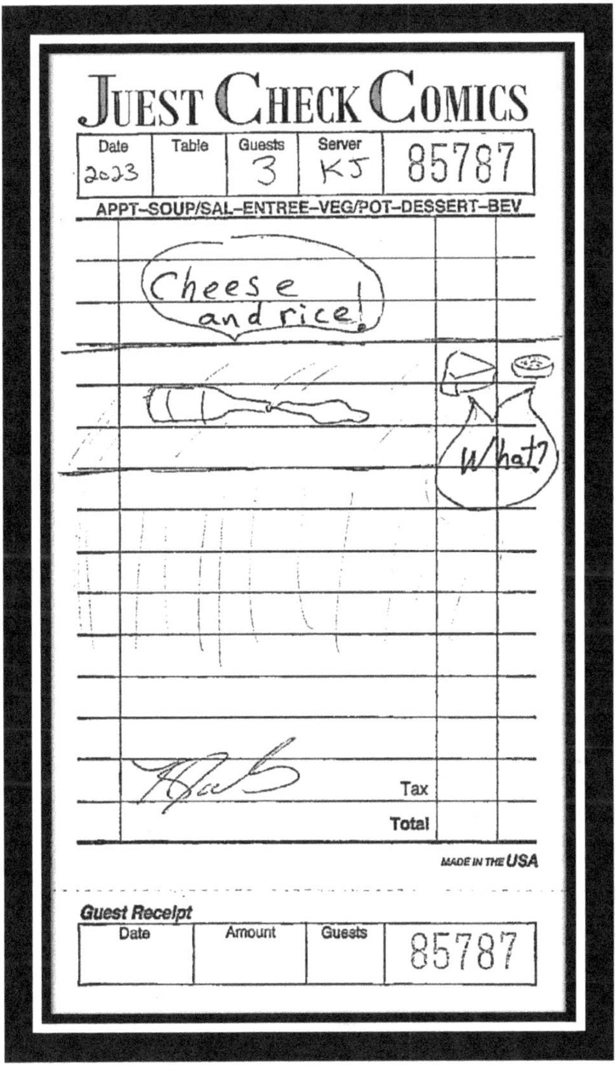
JUEST CHECK COMICS
Date
2023
Table
Guests
3
Server
KJ
85787
APPT–SOUP/SAL–ENTREE–VEG/POT–DESSERT–BEV
Cheese and rice!
What?
Tax
Total
MADE IN THE USA
Guest Receipt
Date
Amount
Guests
85787

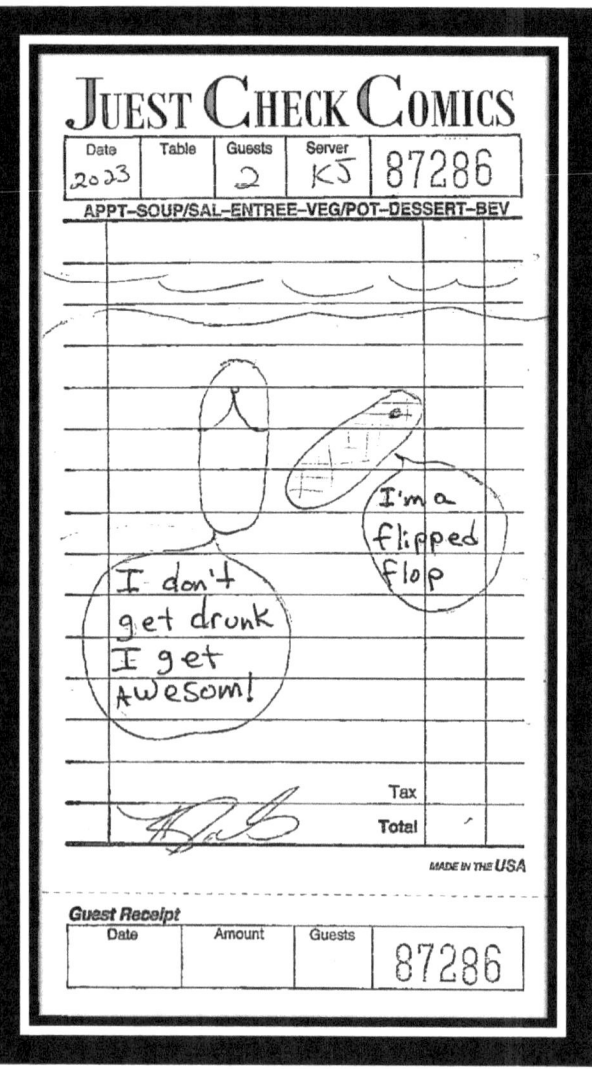

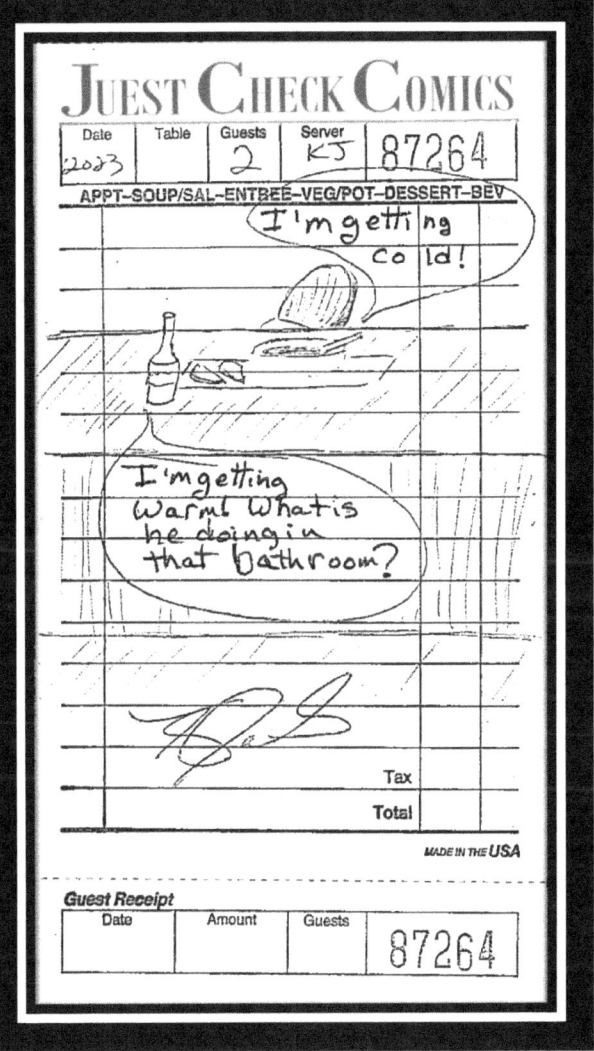

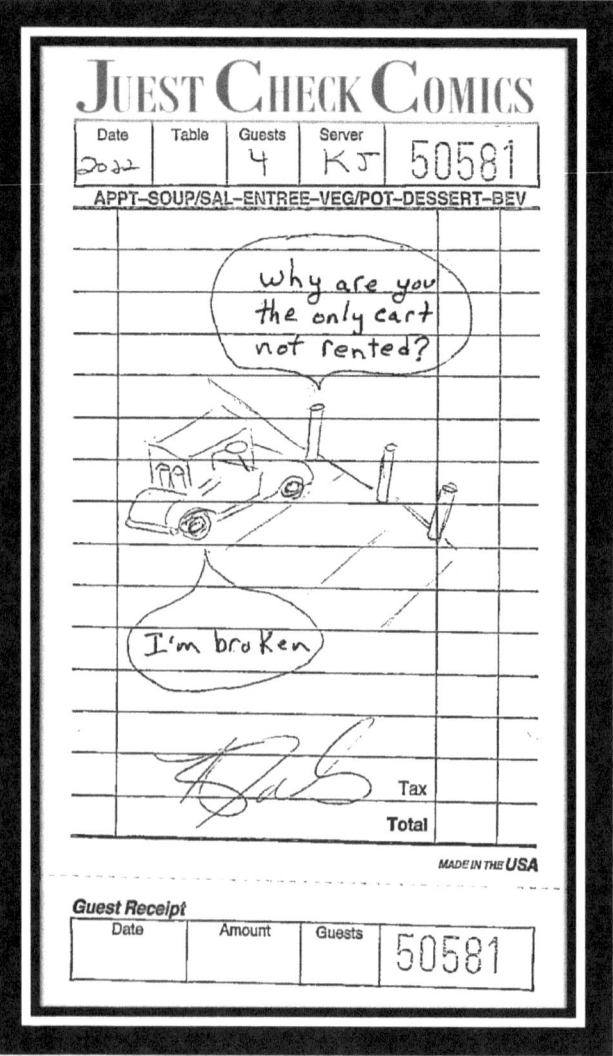

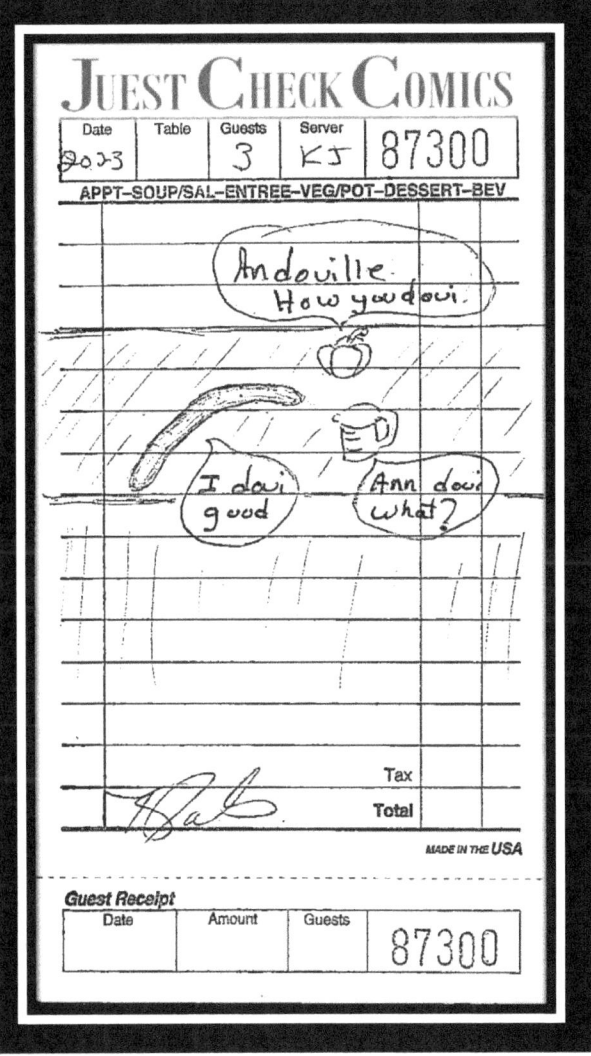

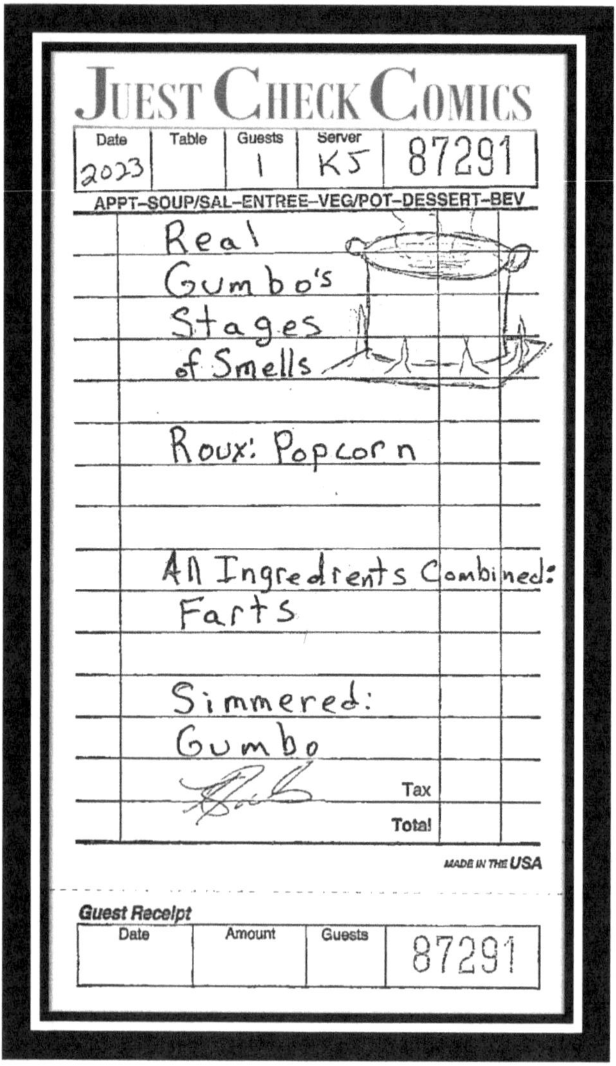
JUEST CHECK COMICS
Date
2023
Table
Guests
1
Server
KS
87291
APPT–SOUP/SAL–ENTREE–VEG/POT–DESSERT–BEV
Real
Gumbo's
Stages
of Smells
Roux: Popcorn
All Ingredients Combined:
Farts
Simmered:
Gumbo
Tax
Total
MADE IN THE USA
Guest Receipt
Date
Amount
Guests
87291

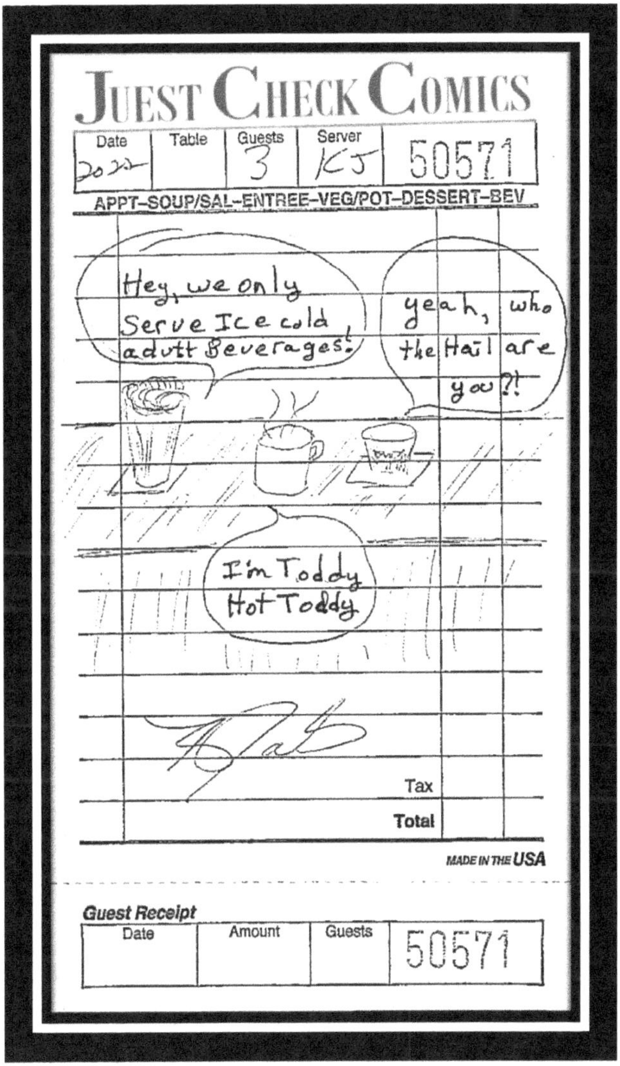
JUEST CHECK COMICS
Date 2022
Table
Guests 3
Server KJ
50571
APPT–SOUP/SAL–ENTREE–VEG/POT–DESSERT–BEV
Hey, we only Serve Ice cold adult Beverages!
yeah, who the Hail are you?!
I'm Toddy Hot Toddy
Tax
Total
MADE IN THE USA
Guest Receipt
Date
Amount
Guests
50571

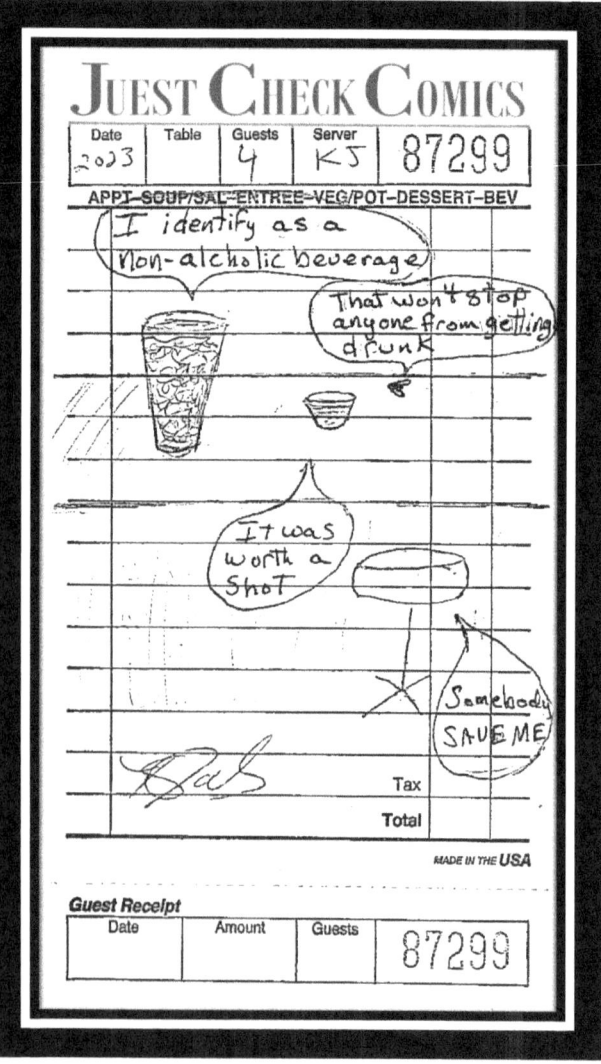

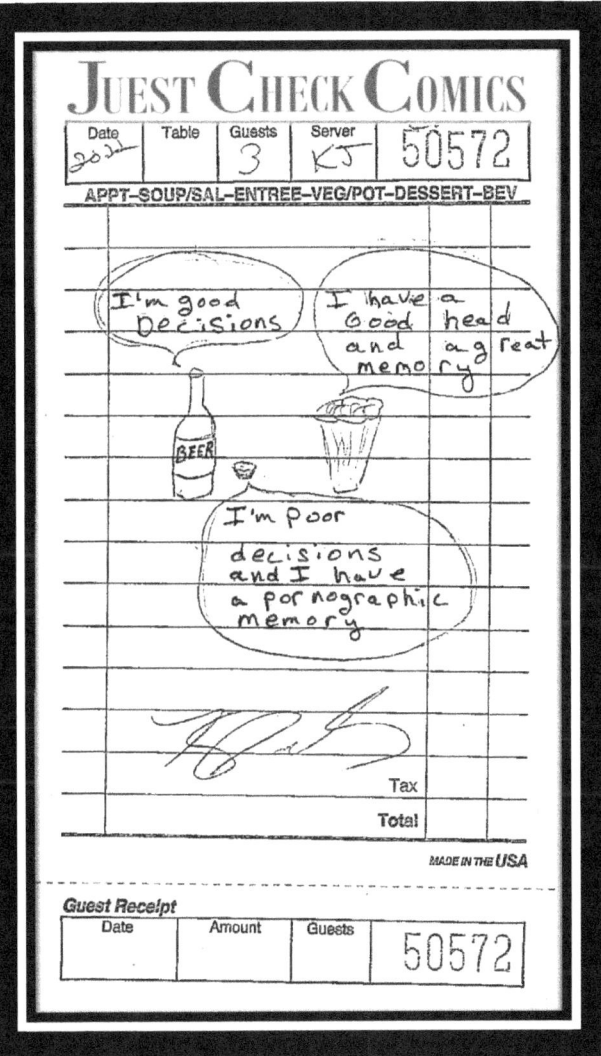

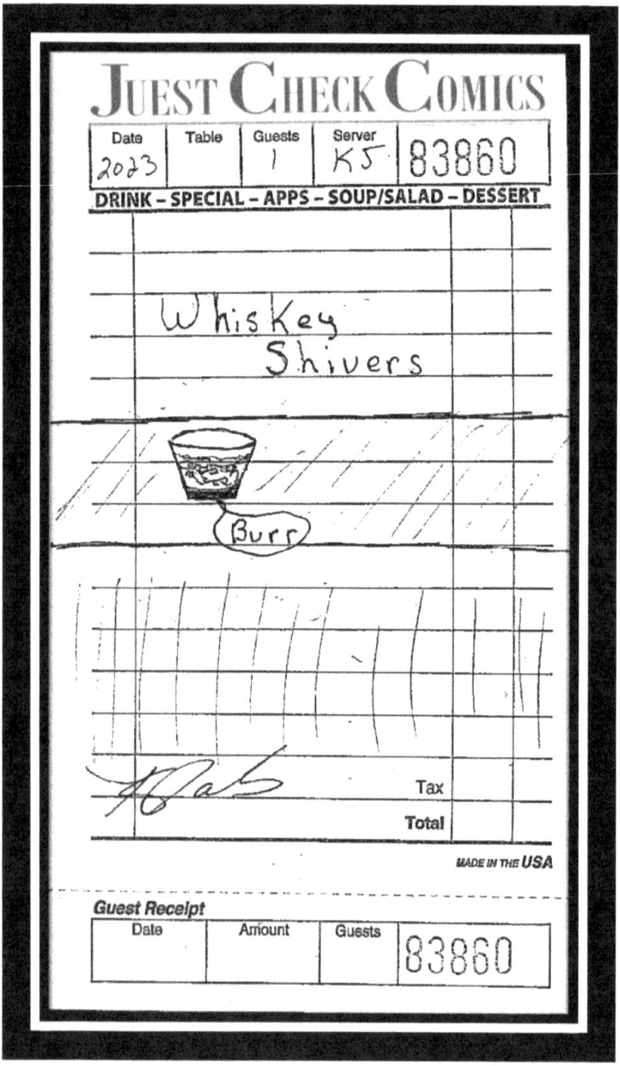
JUEST CHECK COMICS
Date
2023
Table
Guests
1
Server
KS
83860
DRINK – SPECIAL – APPS – SOUP/SALAD – DESSERT
Whiskey Shivers
Burr
Tax
Total
MADE IN THE USA
Guest Receipt
Date
Amount
Guests
83860

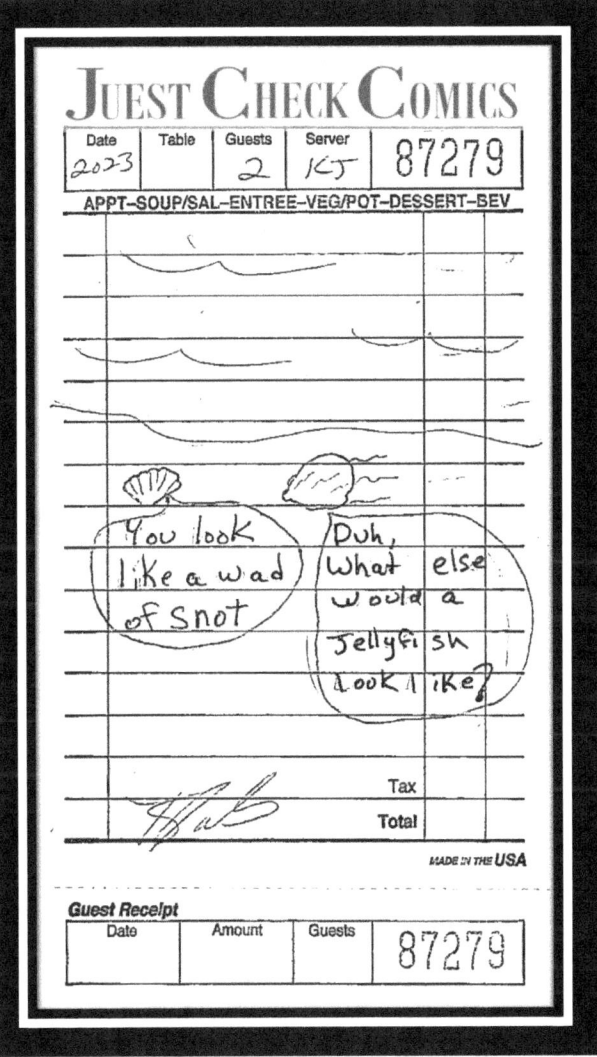

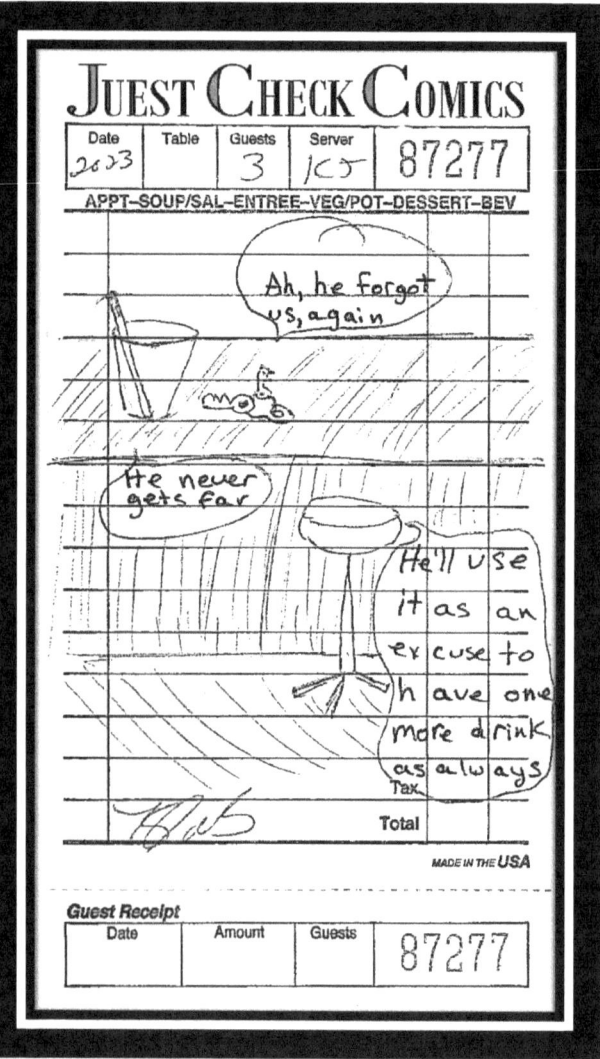

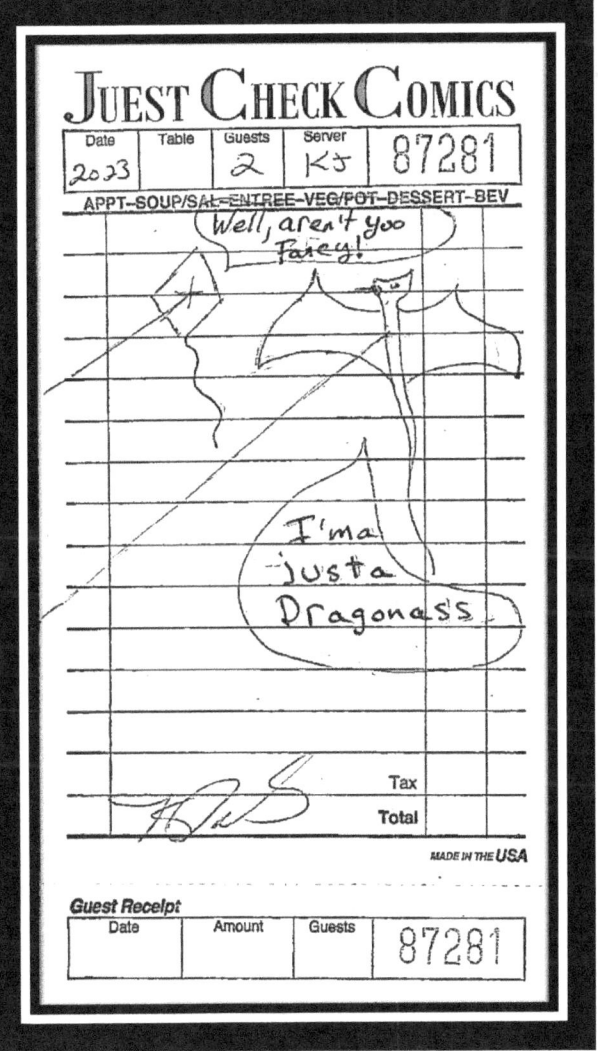

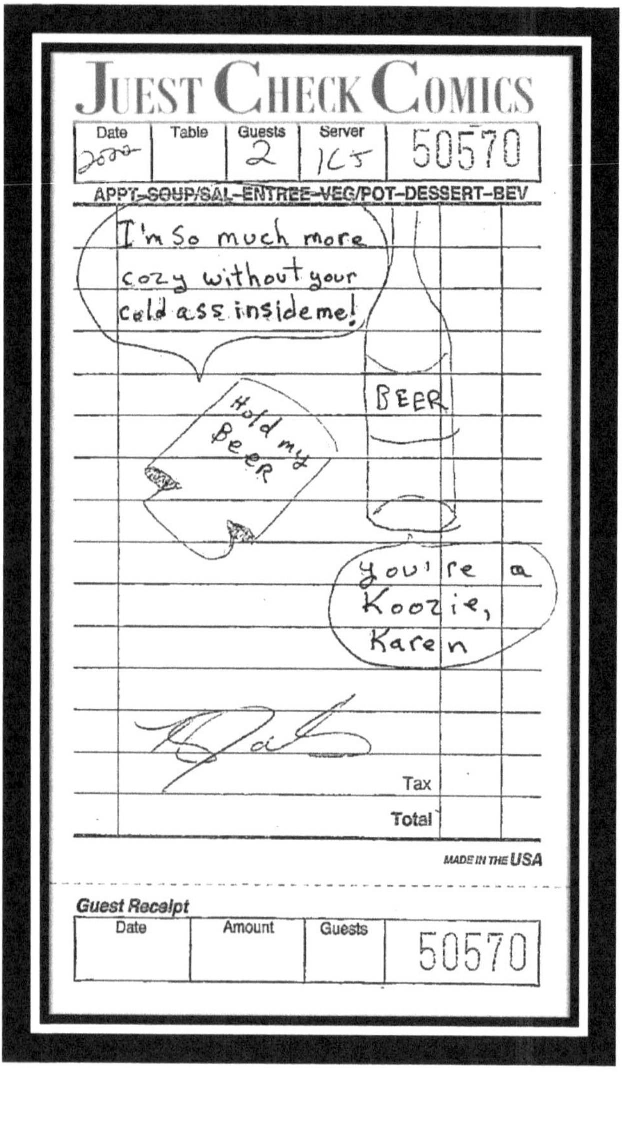
JUEST CHECK COMICS
Date
2022
Table
Guests
2
Server
KS
50570
APPT–SOUP/SAL–ENTREE–VEG/POT–DESSERT–BEV
I'm so much more cozy without your cold ass inside me!
Hold my Beer
BEER
You're a Koozie, Karen
Tax
Total
MADE IN THE USA
Guest Receipt
Date
Amount
Guests
50570

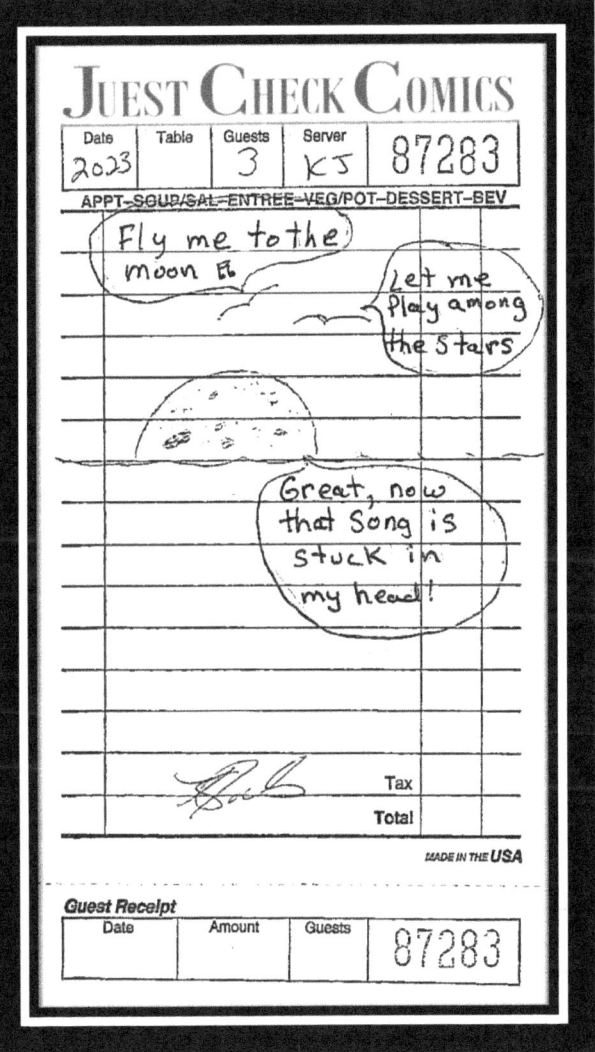

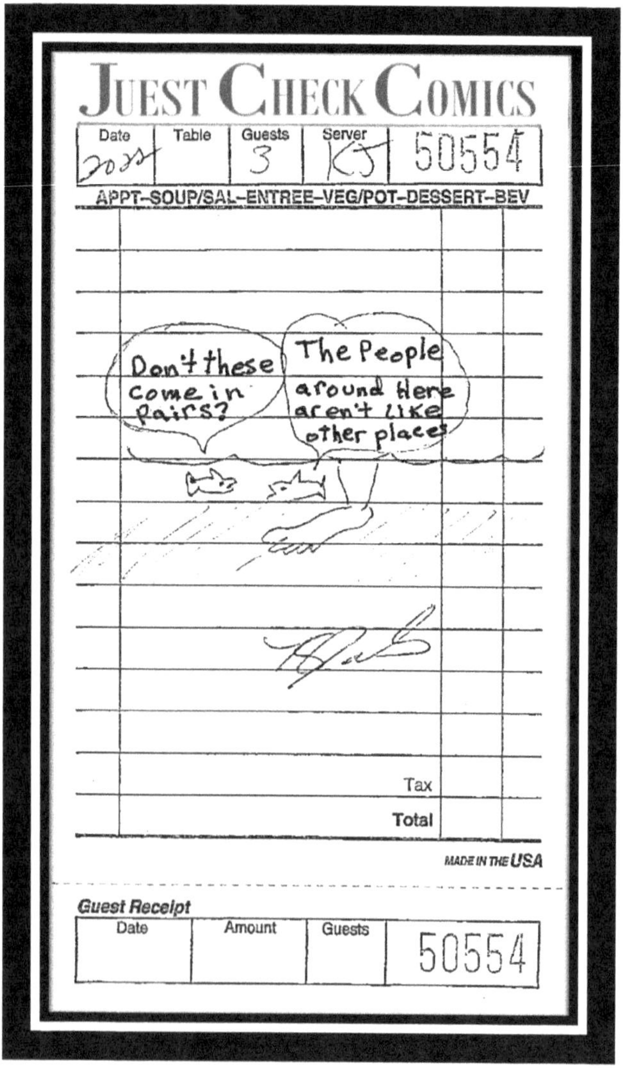
JUEST CHECK COMICS
Date
Table
Guests
Server
3
KJ
50554
APPT–SOUP/SAL–ENTREE–VEG/POT–DESSERT–BEV
Don't these come in pairs?
The People around Here aren't like other places
Tax
Total
MADE IN THE USA
Guest Receipt
Date
Amount
Guests
50554

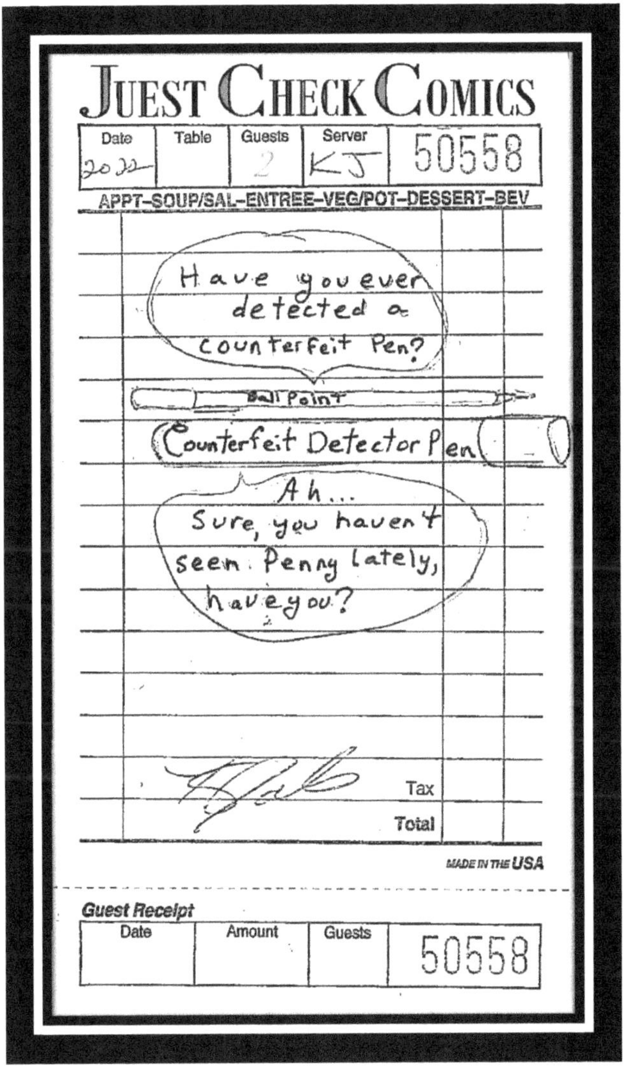
JUEST CHECK COMICS
Date
2022
Table
Guests
2
Server
KJ
50558
APPT–SOUP/SAL–ENTREE–VEG/POT–DESSERT–BEV
Have you ever detected a counterfeit Pen?
Ball Point
Counterfeit Detector Pen
Ah... Sure, you haven't seen Penny lately, have you?
Tax
Total
MADE IN THE USA
Guest Receipt
Date
Amount
Guests
50558

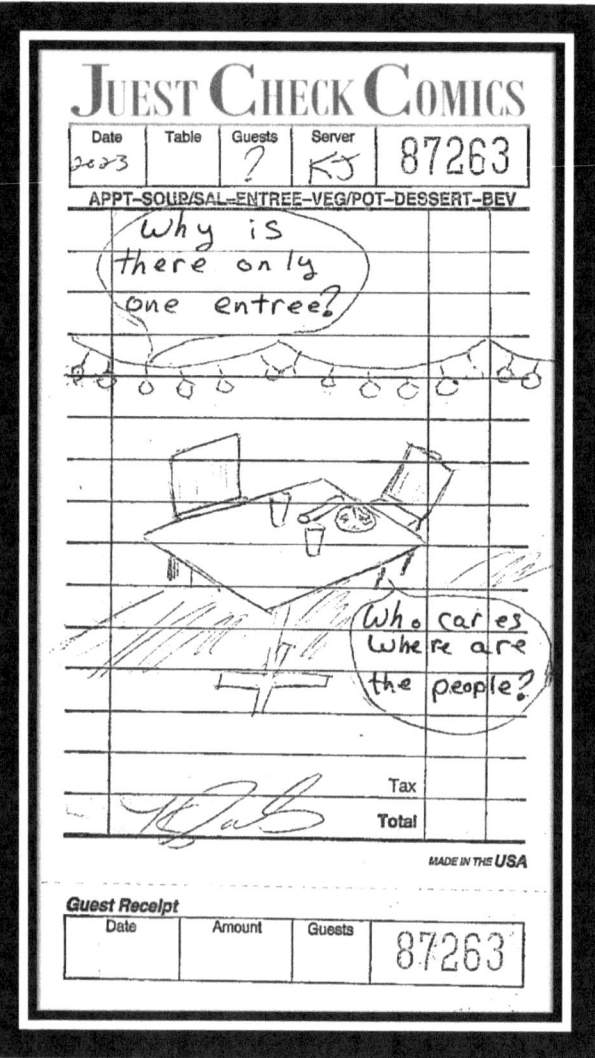

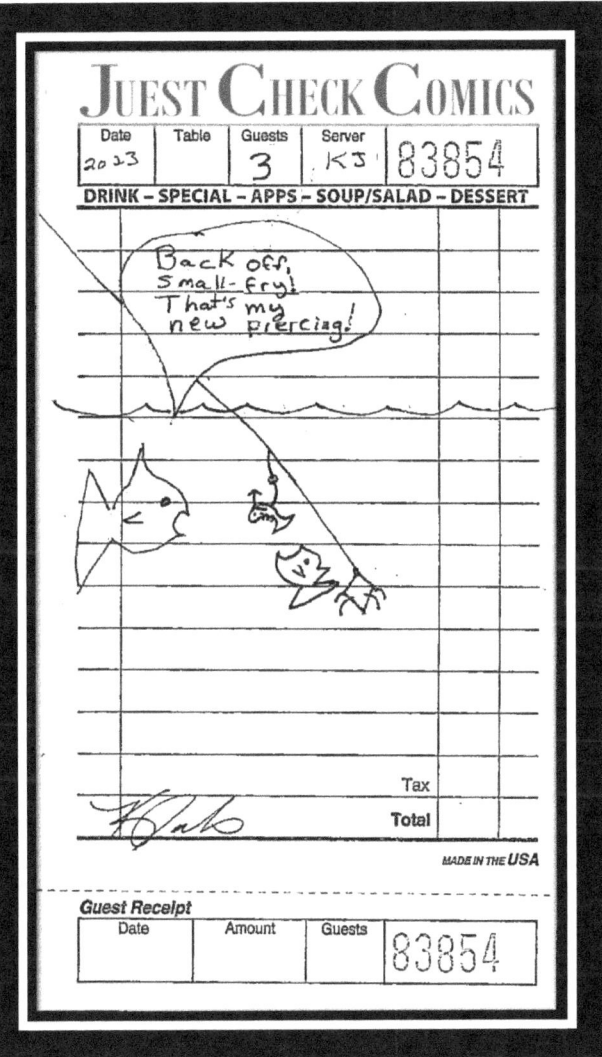

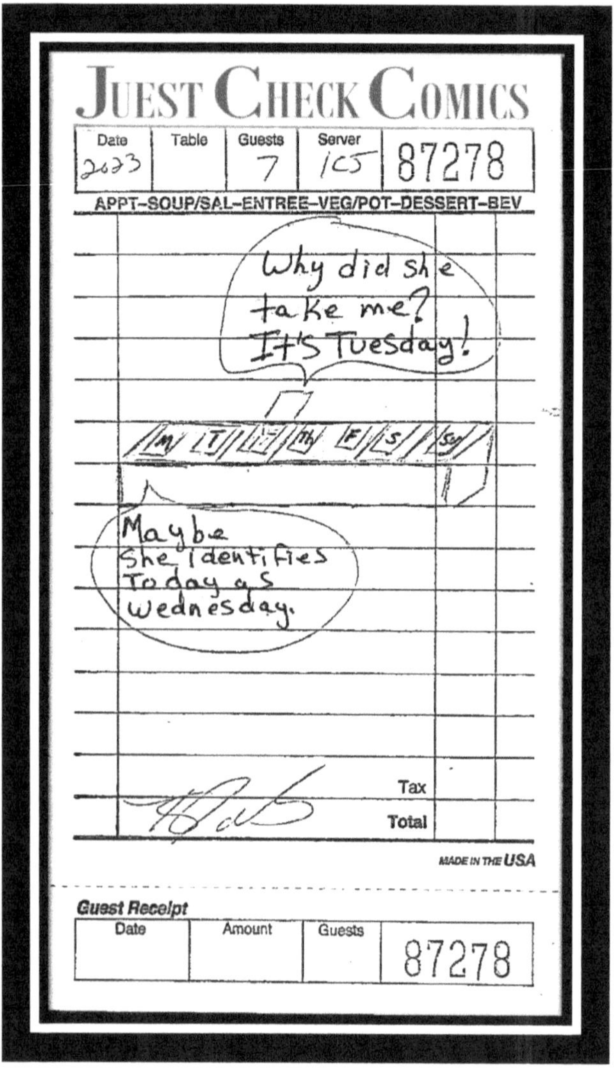
JUEST CHECK COMICS
Date 2023
Table
Guests 7
Server ICS
87278
APPT–SOUP/SAL–ENTREE–VEG/POT–DESSERT–BEV
Why did she take me? It's Tuesday!
Maybe she identifies today as wednesday.
Tax
Total
MADE IN THE USA
Guest Receipt
Date
Amount
Guests
87278

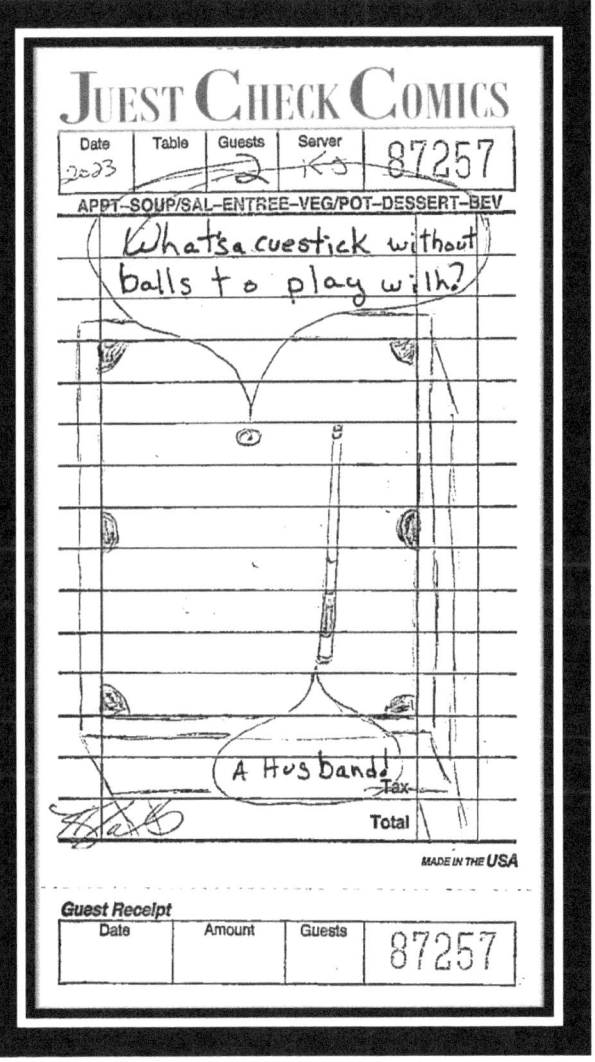

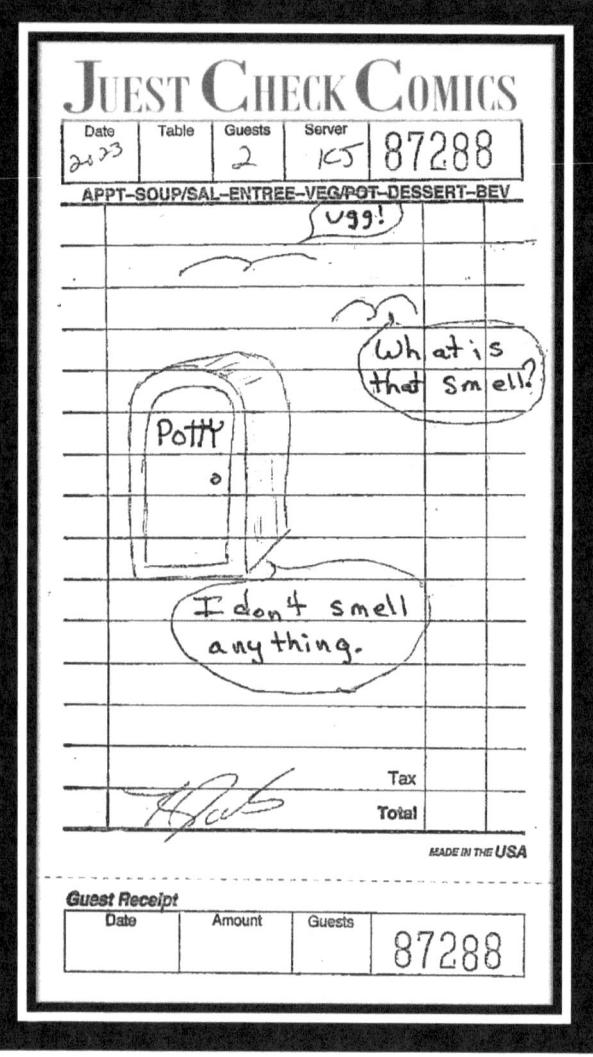

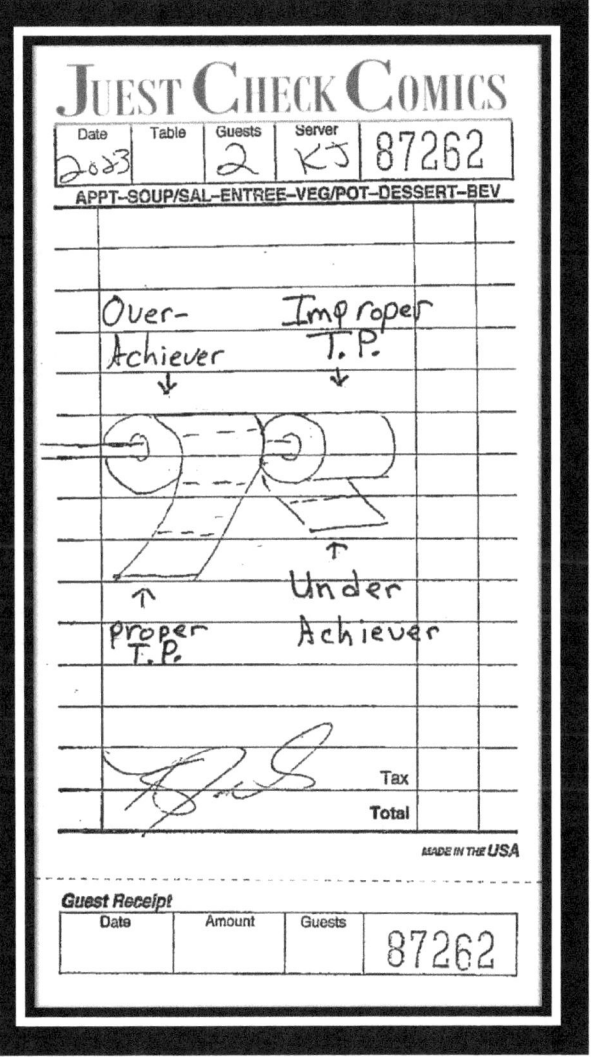

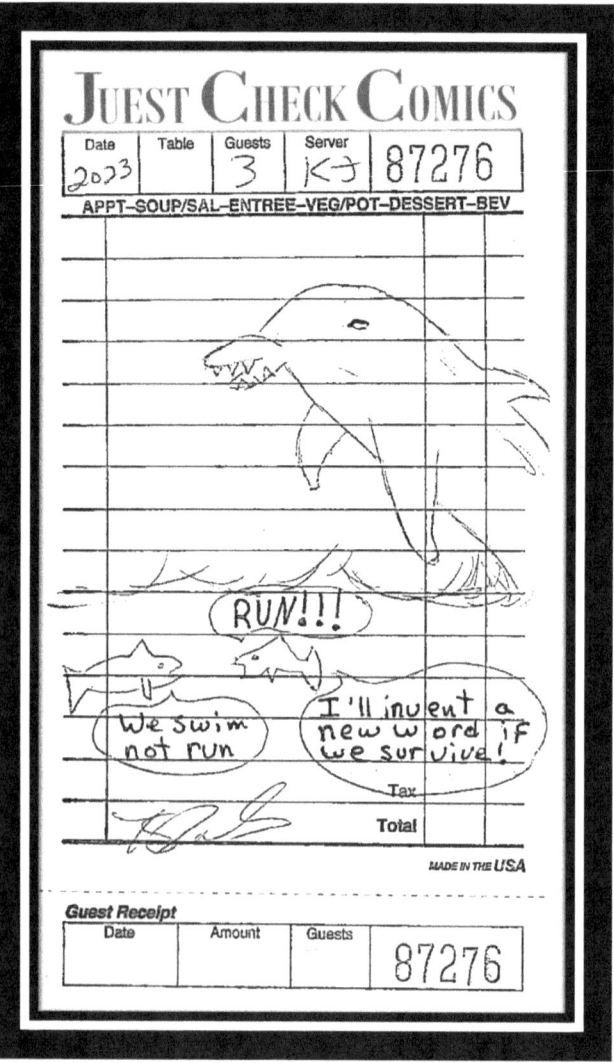

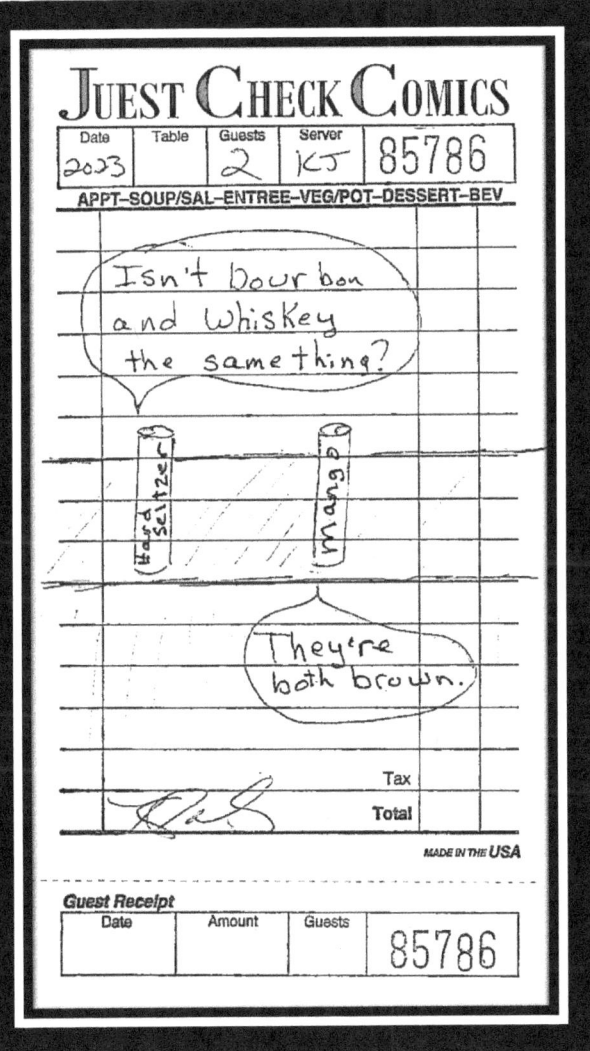

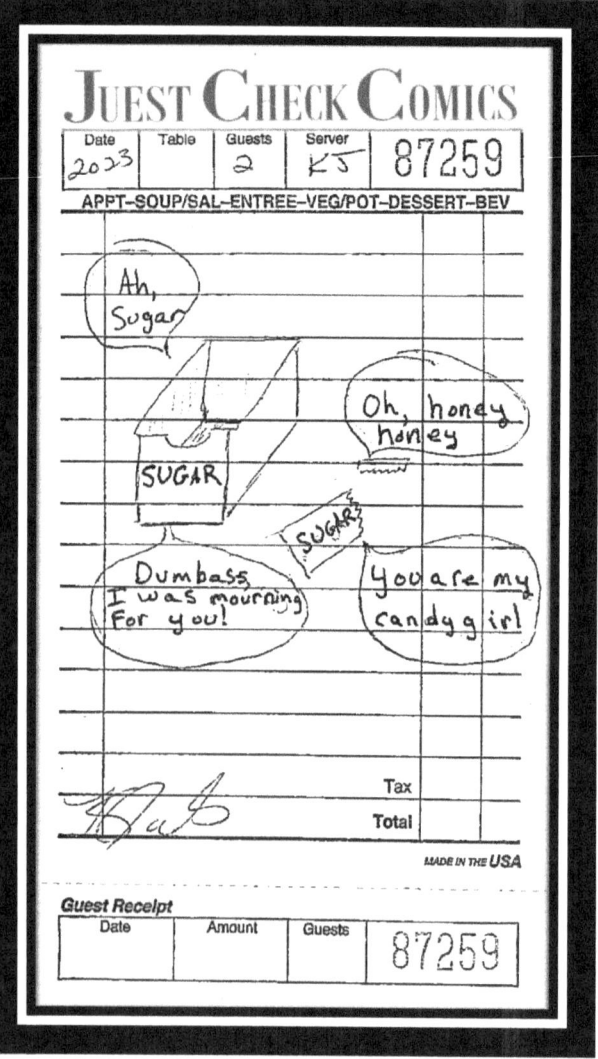

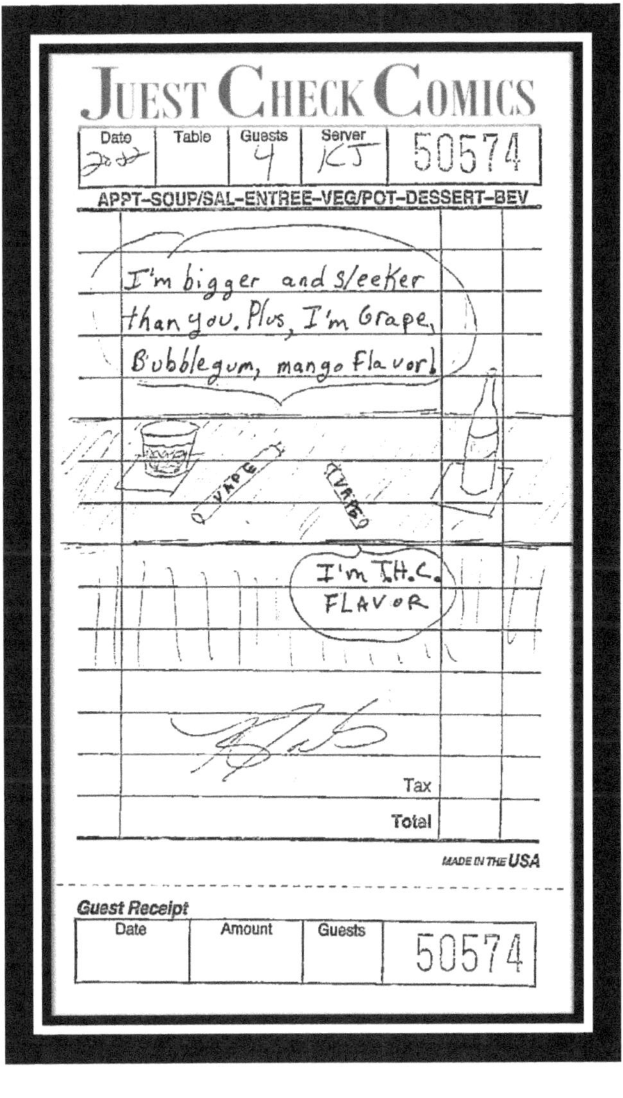
JUEST CHECK COMICS
Date 2022
Table
Guests 4
Server KJ
50574
APPT-SOUP/SAL-ENTREE-VEG/POT-DESSERT-BEV
I'm bigger and sleeker than you. Plus, I'm Grape, Bubblegum, mango flavor!
VAPE
I'm T.H.C. FLAVOR
Tax
Total
MADE IN THE USA
Guest Receipt
Date
Amount
Guests
50574

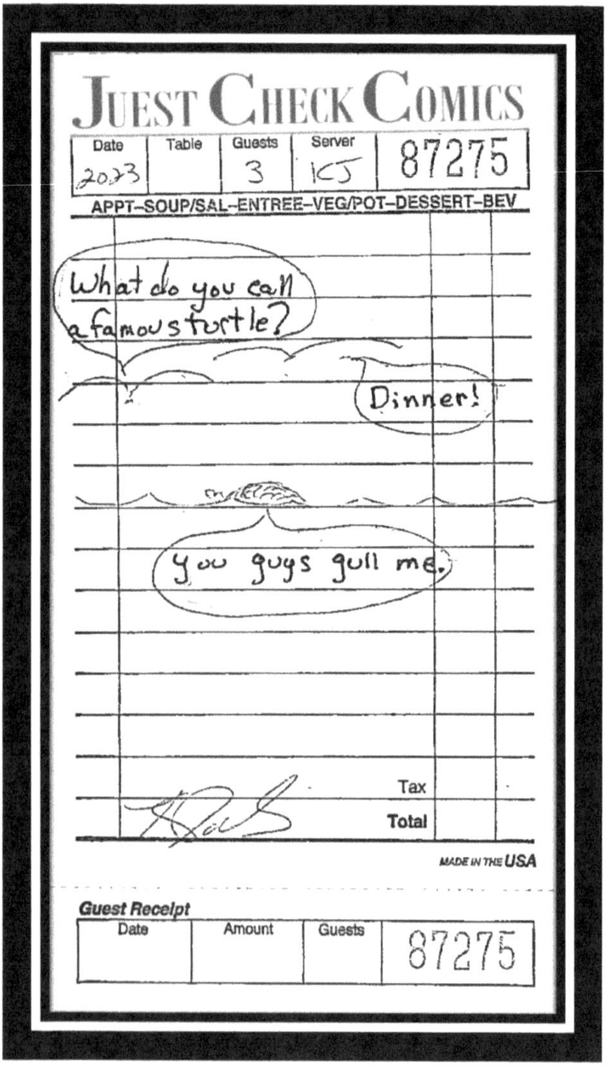
JUEST CHECK COMICS
Date 2023
Table
Guests 3
Server KJ
87275
APPT–SOUP/SAL–ENTREE–VEG/POT–DESSERT–BEV
What do you call a famous turtle?
Dinner!
You guys gull me.
Tax
Total
MADE IN THE USA
Guest Receipt
Date
Amount
Guests
87275

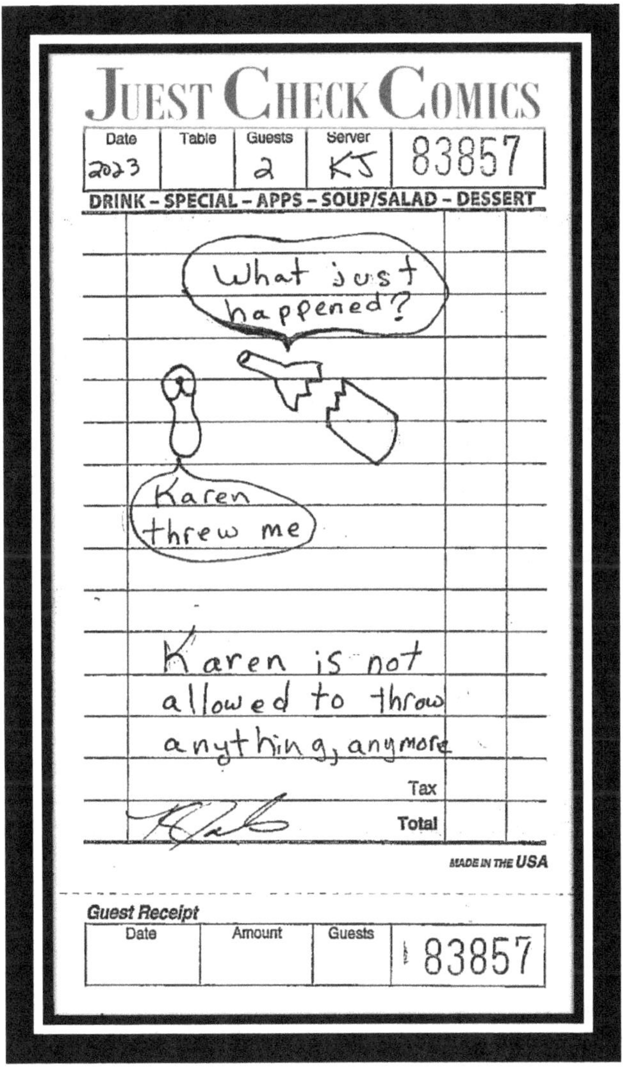
JUEST CHECK COMICS
Date 2023
Table
Guests 2
Server KJ
83857
DRINK – SPECIAL – APPS – SOUP/SALAD – DESSERT
What just happened?
Karen threw me
Karen is not allowed to throw anything, anymore
Tax
Total
MADE IN THE USA
Guest Receipt
Date
Amount
Guests
83857

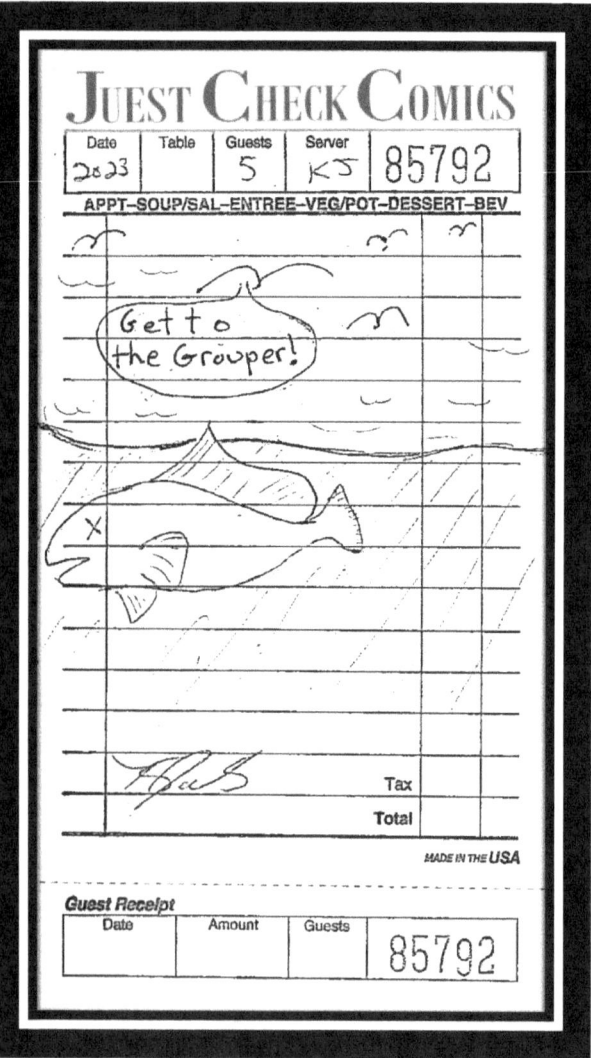

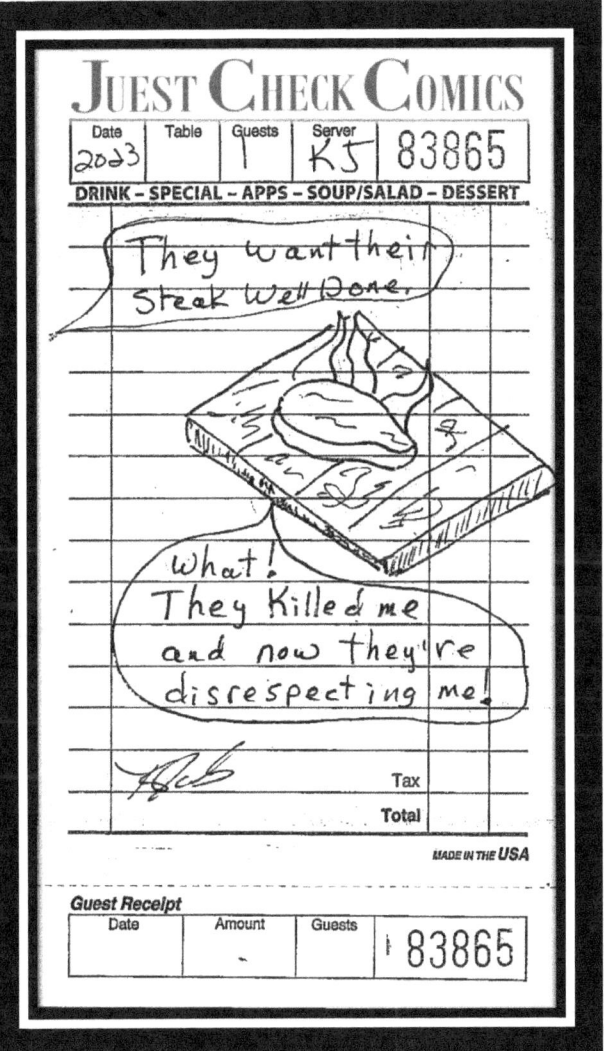

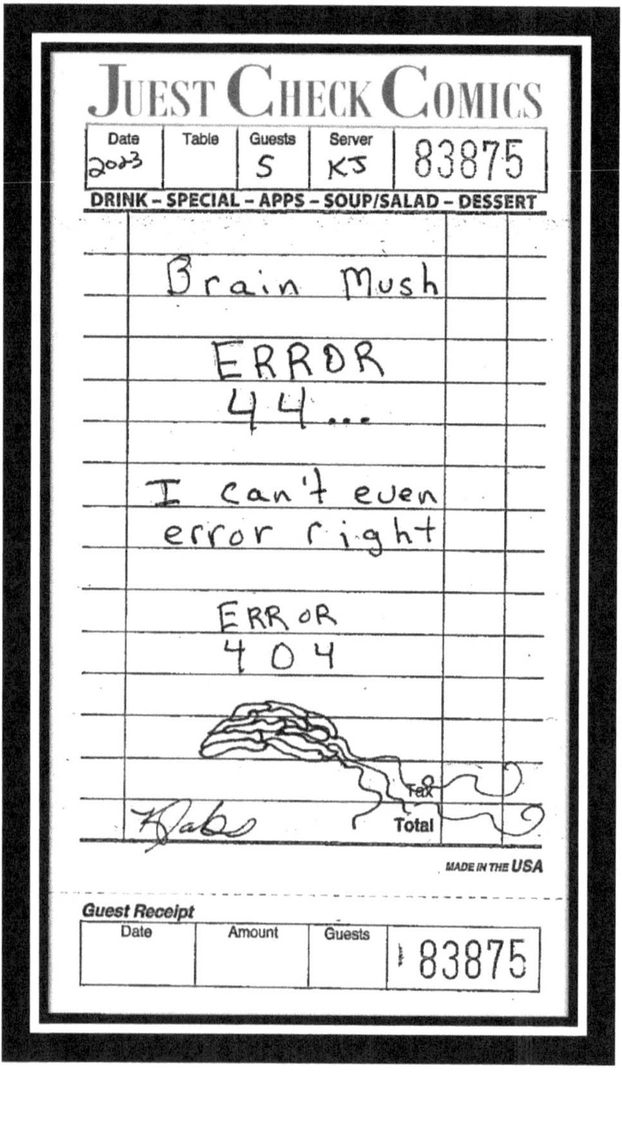
JUEST CHECK COMICS
Date
2023
Table
Guests
5
Server
KJ
83875
DRINK – SPECIAL – APPS – SOUP/SALAD – DESSERT
Brain Mush
ERROR
44...
I can't even
error right
ERROR
404
Tax
Total
MADE IN THE USA
Guest Receipt
Date
Amount
Guests
83875

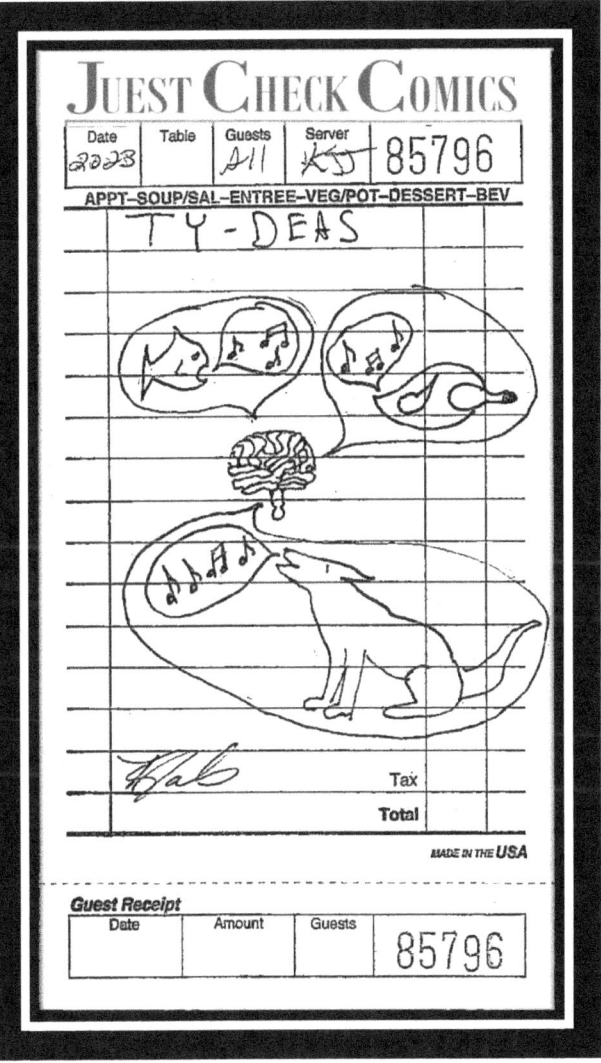

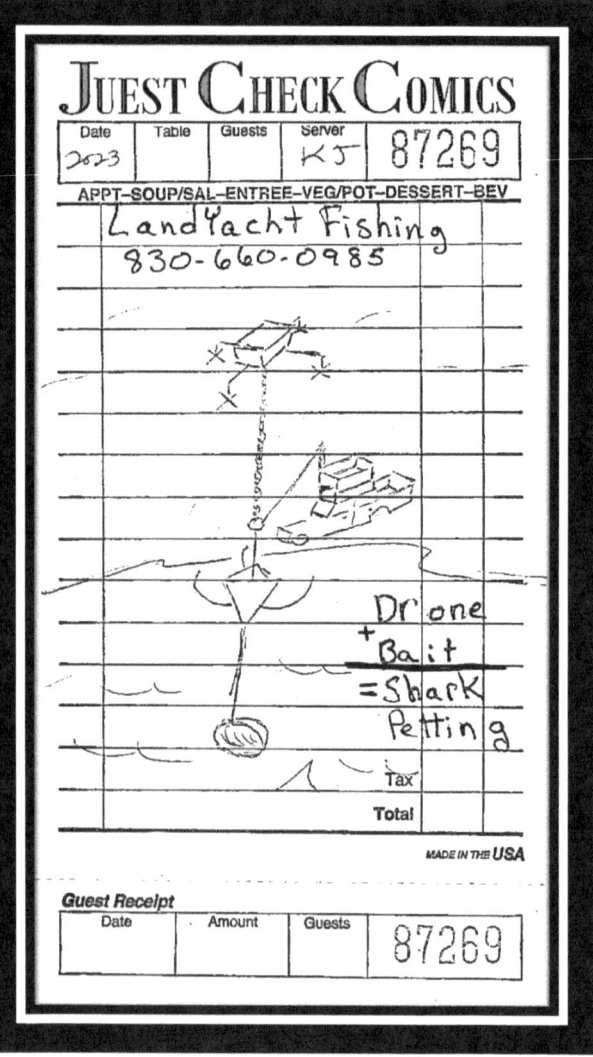

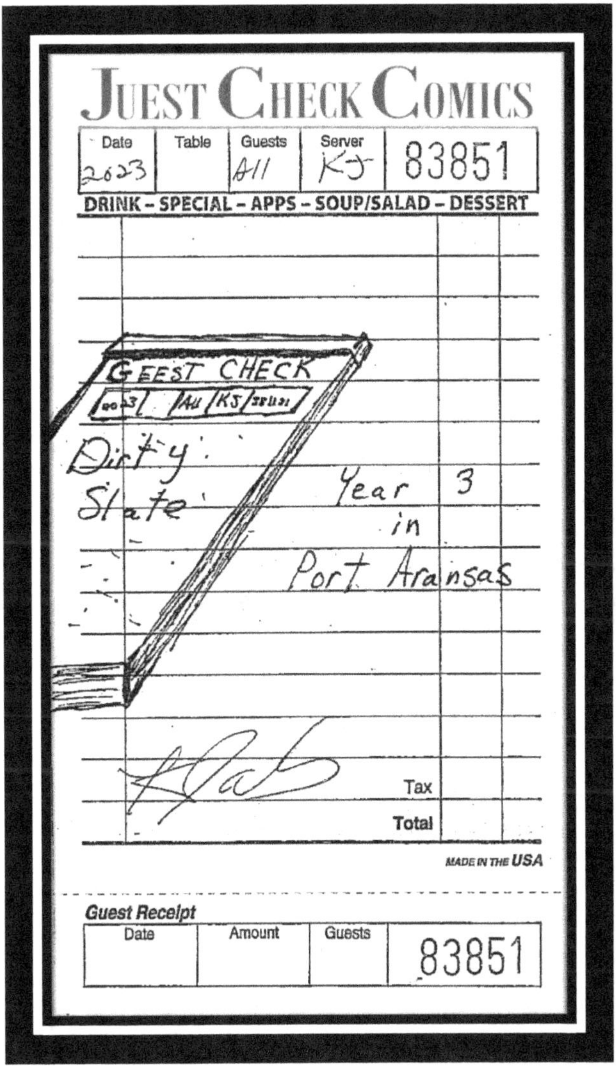
JUEST CHECK COMICS
Date 2023
Table
Guests All
Server KJ
83851
DRINK – SPECIAL – APPS – SOUP/SALAD – DESSERT
GEEST CHECK
Dirty Slate
Year 3 in Port Aransas
Tax
Total
MADE IN THE USA
Guest Receipt
Date
Amount
Guests
83851

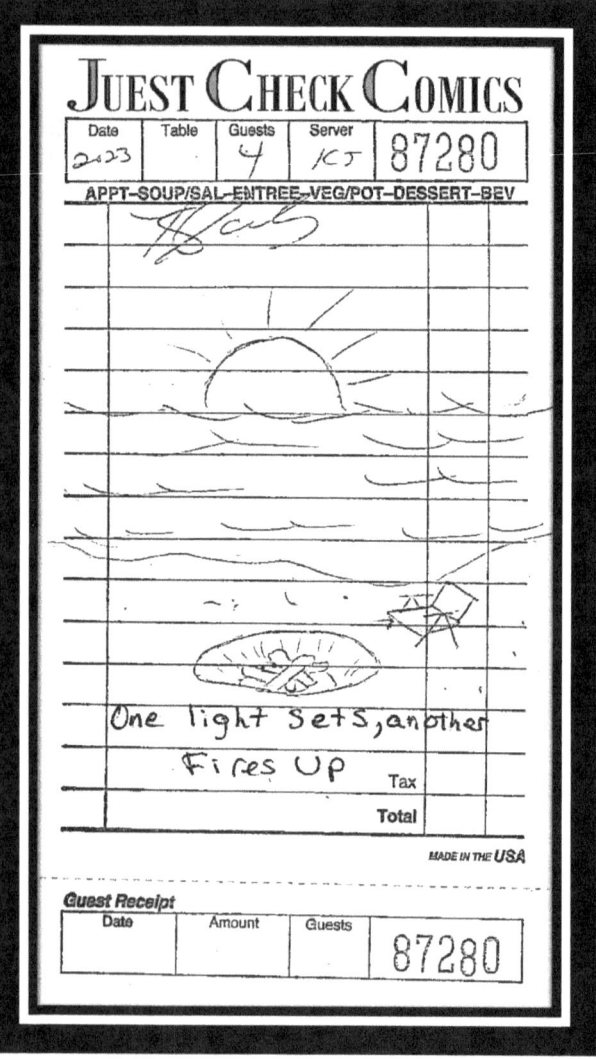

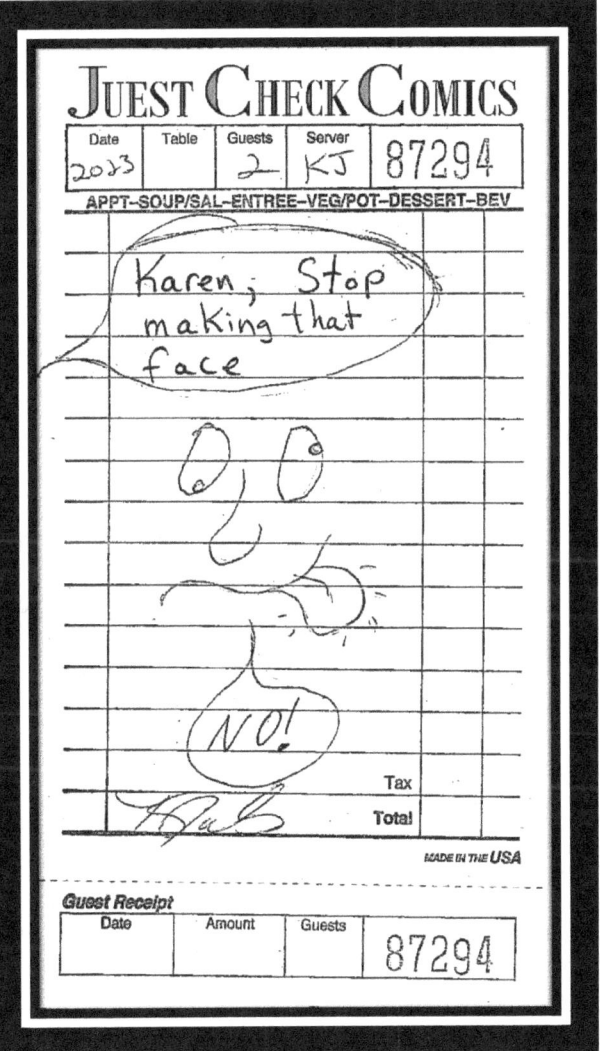

ABOUT THE AUTHOR

"I'm a bitch, I'm a lover, I'm a child, I'm a mother, I'm a sinner, I'm a saint, I do not feel ashamed"… That's one of my anthems. ("Bitch" by Meredith Brooks)

My other is "Basket Case" by Green Day, "Sometimes, I give myself the creeps. Sometimes my mind plays tricks on me. It all keeps adding up, I think I'm cracking up…"

So about me:

Since I was six years old, I've been an aspiring vampire/assassin/mermaid. It wasn't until I was thirteen that I decided to be a writer. Now in adulthood, I'm an accomplished, not yet wildly successful, writer and I love being a bartender, slaying one drink at a time.

The birth of this comic book came about when bartending at Kody's in Port Aransas, Tx during the offseason, (winter.) During slow times, I tried to write on my other book, "Confessions of a Port Aransas Bartender." The minute I'd start, someone would come in, I'd stop writing and I'd lose my groove. It was annoying, but I wasn't paid to be there to write. I began doodling, instead. When I was too busy to doodle, I'd jot down funny things people said at the bar and later come up with a drawing. I'd show these comics to people. When they laughed, giddiness filled me.

I could make people laugh.

If you've read any of my other books, they are not funny. My horror novella, "The Worms Crawl in" scared me enough that I haven't written horror since. "Sometimes my mind gives me the creeps."

"Jolene, You're not a Monster" is an awesome science thriller that inspired me to continue in the thriller genre. My next novel is still collecting dust since my husband of twenty-five years passed.

Comics are so much more fun, anyway. Yes, some are raunchy, inappropriate, but all are light-hearted like the island that inspired them.

If ya haven't visited Port Aransas, I highly recommend our beautiful island with sandy beaches, great fishing, fantastic family friendly activities and exciting not so family friendly nightlife. Oh and we host lots of live music from local musicians and chart toppers.

As you can't tell, I love it here.

Those of you who know Port Aransas, Cheers! Here's to our wonderful Island.

So, till my next volume of comics comes out, may all our lives be on Island Time.

Karen "Kacy Jey" Jacobs

COMING SOON

"Confessions" by Karen "Kacy Jey" Jacobs, exposes life, work and play in Port Aransas. From the crazy, to the silly, to the unbelievably stupid, to the downright assholes, "Confessions," is a trip down the drunken path of us islanders. Join us and experience Mustang Island like a local.

Stories include: The Cunt Man, Ravishing Maben, Cindy and Her Bitch Sister and Blow Job Lady.

If anyone wishes to keep up with Karen's latest works, follow her as Karen A. Jacobs on Facebook or Karen "Kacy Jey" Jacobs on Amazon and Kacy Jey on Facebook.